On Bruce's and Robin's

Bruce and Robin have nurtured three amazing children. The statistical probability of this happening randomly three times without them doing something right is pretty small! — Erica, happy blended: mother of two and stepmother of two

Let's face it: anyone who has raised kids and gotten them into college has learned a thing or two about parenting. It's the ones who are willing to use words like "asshat" that we should be taking advice from because they won't sugarcoat it. — Eric, pastor, YMCA rat, sports fan, and compassionate vomit-cleaner-upper

They've raised daughters, and I've watched them grow through their eyes. I'm currently raising daughters, so any help I can get, I'll take. Plus I respect Bruce a bunch. He really helped me out as I transitioned to adult life. — Dessiree, video editor, mother of two young daughters

Robin and Bruce have somehow raised the most amazing girls. They are strong, powerful, creative, intelligent, and caring. Years ago, I asked them to write a parenting book so that I could learn how to be parents like them. I am so glad they listened. I can only hope my young girls turn out to be as awesome as theirs. — Angie, sweet potato artist, mother of two, educator, problem solver, and finder

The first time I had a professional meeting with Bruce, he brought two of his girls. They sat at the next table in the coffee shop, and I watched them as much as I listened to him. It seemed a miracle—a professional man integrating work and family. I wanted to be able to do that too. I learned as much from him and Robin (and their extended family) about family, parenting, and love as I learned about being a pastor. —Abby, mom of two stuck in the Midwest dreaming about California and its coffee

Robin and Bruce have raised three wonderful talented daughters. They have done this while admitting their mistakes from time to time. Their humility and transparency have taught the same skills to their daughters. Plus they don't take themselves too seriously. —Mark, chaplain, polity geek, experienced as a child of two parents

Life is easier when you are surrounded by family, friends, and neighbors. If you're lucky enough to find Bruce and Robin in your circle, you are truly blessed (and well fed). Truly an amazing couple who share a passionate commitment to raising loving, thoughtful, socially aware children. A must read. —Mary, nurse and mother

Bruce and Robin are fantastic parents because their children (namely their oldest daughter) have turned out so great. She really is wonderful. —Evelyn, uprooted college kid trying to be an adult while living in a loft bed

Rule #2: Don't Be an Asshat

An Official Handbook for
Raising Parents and Children

by Robin Pugh and Bruce Reyes-Chow 06/10

#42, #61, #81 *Bruce Reyes-Chow*

#3, #27, #100 *Robin Pugh*

For information:
Bacosa Books
1728 Ocean Avenue, #203
San Francisco, CA 94112
Or contact us online at www.bacosabooks.com
Book design by Bruce Reyes-Chow
Edited by Laura Garwood
Cover design by Adam Walker Cleaveland

Dear, _____ ____/____/____

I am giving you this parenting handbook because:* _____

_____

_____

_____

_____

_____

_____

_____

_____

*** Disclaimer:*** While well-timed sass, cutting snark, and the occasional passive-aggressive barb make for good TV, the authors are not responsible for any advice, counsel, or suggestions offered by the giver of this book.

_____

We dedicate this book to…

Evelyn, who has been with us from the beginning,

Abby, who is not one of them invisible middle kids,

and Annie, who has to spend two years by herself with us.

You remind us every day

to love the life that we've been given,

to have the courage to be ourselves,

and to giggle like middle schoolers.

Thank you.

FAMILY SELFIE, 2015

Table of Contents

Rule #41: Kiss your lola (Dad) **69**

Rule #42: Have faith (Dad) **70**

Rule #43: Protest (Dad) **71**

Rule #44: Giggle like a middle schooler (Dad) **72**

Rule #45: Never lie to your doctor (Mom) **73**

Rule #46: Don't mock (Dad) **74**

Rule #47: Talk about the sex (Mom) **75**

Rule #48: Have good sex (Dad) **76**

Rule #49: Be a good leader (Dad) **77**

Rule #50: Be a good follower (Dad) **78**

Rule #51: Find your people (Mom) **79**

Rule #52: Be self-reflective (Dad) **80**

Rule #53: Clap when they can't hear you (Dad) **81**

Rule #54: Never lose hope (Dad) **82**

Rule #55: Remember others (Dad) **83**

Rule #56: Play board games (Mom) **84**

Rule #57: Look homeless people in the eye (Mom) **85**

Rule #58: Be cute, strong, and smart (Dad) **86**

Rule #59: Be adventurous (Dad) **87**

Rule #60: Forge your own path (Mom) **88**

Add your own... **89**

Rule #61: Read for fun (Dad) **90**

Rule #62: Watch baseball (Dad) **91**

Rule #63: Be political (Mom) **92**

Rule #64: Hold babies and attend funerals (Dad) **93**

Rule #65: Scream as needed (Dad) **94**

Rule #66: Watch silly movies (Dad) **95**

Rule #67: You do you online (Dad) **96**

FAMILY, 2004

Kickstarter Dedications

This book project was made possible only through the generosity of our friends, our community, and a few strangers who choose to invest in #DontBeAnAsshat. A few folks backed the project through Kickstarter at a level where they received the "reward" of leaving a dedication for loved ones.

My dedication goes to those who helped nurture and inspire my parenting style: my parents, Steve and Marie; my husband, Joel; and my very special, unique children, who taught me patience, openness, and the importance of unconditional love.—**Sarah Reyes**

To Angela Kothe and Mitchell Kothe, a must-read for when you become parents!—**Louise Kothe**

Dedicated to all those who helped me to grow into a parent who (#crossingfingers) isn't an asshat.—**Barbara Nixon**

Thanks to these folks, and to the rest of those who backed this Kickstarter project. I have no doubt that, together, we will turn back the tides of asshattery!

Sisters, 2003

The Origin Story

The impetus for writing this book came from our friend Jenn Owens. She posted a Facebook update in response to an incident at a local pool with her daughter, Koi, pleading to the parenting universe:

I rarely (if ever) give parenting "advice" on Facebook…mainly because I'm NO role model. I'm often lazy, lose my temper over stupid shit, and seem to have poor judgment when Koi is sick (I either underreact or overreact). But I always try to teach her to be kind to people (well, she naturally is anyway). I try to teach her to follow the rules: wait your turn, never ever express anger through violence, and don't take other people's stuff—that sort of thing.

With that being said, I feel as a parent, we have ONE job with our kids: NOT TO RAISE ASSHOLES. Why is that so hard? Please enlighten me—what are the benefits of raising children to grow up to be selfish jerks?

Enlighten me. What is the benefit of raising kids who are assholes, who will later grow up to be adults who are assholes. Please educate me on the benefits of asshole-itry. Thank you for listening. And good night.

After reading that post from Jenn, we were inspired. You see, not only is the asshole's cousin the "asshat," one of Bruce's favorite words of all time, but also Jenn is absolutely correct in her plea to all parents and raisers of children. It really does seems so simple, yet we know it is not.

Parenting is chaotic, messy, and filled with emotional landmines just waiting for unsuspecting parents to explode with one misstep and banishall parties to assholedom for all eternity. At the same time, we know that most kids are not, in fact, being raised to be assholes. We choose to believe that most children have parental and communal influences that are doing their best to raise humans who are kind, compassionate, and just. It's just that in the chaos and muck of life, there are times when we could all use a little help.

So it is with great joy that we offer a big bag of thanks to Jenn for inspiring us to take on this project. She has challenged us to think about who we are as parents and to be courageous and confident enough to put to paper our best ideas that may address her initial call not to raise assholes—or asshats.

Introduction

We have all been there. Whether it was the first day you realized that you were responsible for raising a tiny human person or the first time that growing human person expressed their right to defiance and sassery, in the most daunting of parenting moments, you may have reached out into the abyss, grasping for that "official parenting handbook" that would soothe your spirits with words of guidance, reassurance, or vindication. To be able to say, just one time, when your teenager's "tone" turned from delightful to demonic, "You know it says right here in the official parenting handbook that you should turn down the sass" — and then be able to actually pull out a copy and show them; this is a parental dream. And this is what we are providing you with this handbook.

Yeah, yeah, yeah, we know what you are thinking: "You know what the world needs today? Another gosh darned parenting book." Calm down, Sassy McSasserston, because in all honesty, we kinda feel the same way. With the naive optimism of a teenage boy in the '80s who thought,

"All Molly Ringwald has to do is meet me, and she will totally want to date me," we hope to go beyond filling your mind with impossible, pious, or laughable advice. Our intention is that this handbook and our 101 rules will actually help you parent.

Like many parents, especially with the first kid, we have read book after book after book on how to be good parents. We have tackled healthy eating practices, ideal sleep patterns, homeopathic medicine, attachment parenting, cosleeping, socially conscious shopping, diaper choices, and so on and so on. We withheld refined sugar for two years, we boycotted any shoes made in China, we forbade Barbies from entering our home, and on more than one occasion we carried luggage that included week-old poop-filled cloth diapers making their arduous trek home for washing.

So yeah, we've tried some things that worked really well and other things that were well intentioned but utter failures and/or eye roll worthy. Our parents, aunts, uncles, siblings, and pretty much anyone else upon whom we subjected our parenting diatribes and ideals had most impressive self-control.

There was very little public mockery.

Key word: "public."

Now, don't get us wrong; we do believe that it's important to lean into any and all resources that may improve one's parenting, but for most of this adventure, truth be told *shhhhhhhh*—we've been making things up as we go. Constantly wading through the murky waters of the "nature versus nurture" sea, we do our best, we sometimes stumble and then stumble again, we get back up, and we keep trying. Along the way, we hope that we don't merely provide food, clothes, and shelter, but that we also shape and form human beings who are kind, who are compassionate, and who will make a difference in the world.

No pressure.

We find comfort in the fact that people have been raising kids for a very long time, and parents of each generation did what they could do with the information they had at the time. In other words, they also made it up as they went along. And I am willing to bet they did so without buying any parenting books, navigating the ever-changing rules about car seats, or being able to google, "How do I remove a flash drive from my toddler's nose?" In the case of our parents there was smoking while pregnant (Robin's), coming home from hospital in the footwell of the car (Bruce's), and a couple of nasty divorces (both of ours).

And as they say, "We turned out all right."

So why bother with our version of the parenting handbook? And by what right are we contributing to the ever-growing industrial complex of parenting punditry? Or to ask it another way, "Why the h-e-double-hockey-sticks are you, Bruce Steven Charles Reyes-Chow and Robin Elaine Pugh, at all qualified to write a parenting book?"

Valid question.

Here are a few reasons, a couple of clarifications, and a few experiences that make us feel confident in offering counsel.

Firstly, despite the reality that we are all parenting imposters at some level, none of us should take on the challenge without any guidance. Yes, we jump in and learn to swim, but we should do our best to always have the edge of the pool within an arm's reach, and maybe even take a few swimming lessons along the way. In the same way, we think we have some helpful ideas and guidance for you to hold on to and a few lessons to pass on as you fumble around in the turbulent waters of parenthood.

Secondly, after nearly twenty years of parenting daughters who are now ages nineteen (Evelyn), fifteen (Abby), and thirteen (Annie), we have a veritable laboratory in which we mad-scientist parents have been testing out our parenting ideas.

Bwahahahahahah.

After surviving these first stages of our parenting journey, we want to share a bit about ways in which we embody the worldview in which we raise our kids. We believe this worldview has helped them to thrive in body, mind, and spirit—and is challenging and equipping them to be people who impact the world in positive and meaningful ways.

Thirdly, while we have no advanced degrees in early childhood development, family systems, or child psychology, we are raising three daughters, and we have been intentional about creating a healthy family system, expressing appropriate individual expectations, and engaging in communal culture. We believe that we have offered them the guidance, structures, and community that will help them them to make good choices in life as they explore an ever-expanding world and grow into a positive, caring, and content human beings.

Fourthly—if there is such a word—we'd like to share a quick word about about our faith. While we are far from fundamentalist Bible launchers, our parenting is infused with, grounded in, and informed by our Christian tradition. We are both Presbyterians who believe in a faith that demands of us grace, faith, justice, hope, compassion, and love. This in no way means that we are bait-and-switching you into reading a "Christian parenting" book. In fact, we firmly believe that those of other faith traditions or no faith tradition at all can be just as awful or as wonderful parentals as we Christians can be. Just as no other faith tradition has cornered the market on positive ways to approach marriage, social issues, politics, or parenting, neither have Christianity or we Christian types. This will be the one of the few times that we will reference our faith, but we didn't want you to find out later and think that we were somehow trying to sneak the sweet little baby Jesus by you.

Fifthly—yes, this is getting ridiculous now—if you have not figured it out by now, while this book is framed around passing on life lessons and life hacks to the children in our world, it is also meant to be a set of reminders about how we as adults should live in the world. Sure, you adults will have your own wisdom to add, but in the end, the morals and virtues that we hope to instill are the ones that we hope to model ourselves *and* to see in others around us. We are not always successful, but when committed to raising our children with a particular way of seeing and living in the world, we are constantly reminded that we must do our best to do the same.

Finally, at some point you should expect to experience a range of emotions. Like you do in life in general and parenting in particular, as you read, we hope that you will laugh out loud, wipe away an unexpected tear, experience affirmation, be prodded by a challenge, and on the rare occasion, throw the book across the room screaming, "This handbook is a pile of [bleeping] [bleep]!" As we will talk about later, we are all different: the communities in which we live, the experiences that form us, the passions that give our lives texture, and most important, the ways in which we experience the endeavor of parenting. We know that you will not agree with everything we say, but we hope that there is enough here that will help form and inform your own perspectives and practices so that you, your children, your family, and the world will be better from having been exposed to our story.

What you have in your hands are our greatest words of guidance, wisdom, and help that we hope to pass on to our kids—and really, all other children in the world. It will not resonate with everyone, but it is the handbook that we have chosen to follow ourselves, and we hope that it will aid you as you too raise the children who grace your world.

So thank you for taking the time to hear us out and to join us in this sometimes excruciating, often chaotic, and generally lovely journey of parenting—we hope this helps.

Parents, Children, and "Family"

Never fear—we will get to the list of rules, but we also want to be sure that we lay out a few assumptions that we hold as we discuss "parenting" and the cast of characters involved in the real-life drama of raising children today.

So about what we consider "family." Well, obviously family has only one meaning: one mother, one father, one daughter, one son, ½ of another child, a playful puppy or an aloof cat, and weekends spent blissfully skipping through the park, picking daisies and swinging your 2½ children by the arms. The wondrous day in the life of a "regular" family is topped off by a raucous, breadstick-driven, and ravioli-filled meal at the local faux Italian eating establishment.

Oh, wait, are you gagging just a bit?

No worries—us too.

We all know that families come in all forms and flavors. In fact, in our experience, there are more families who do not fit the traditional definitions than those who do. Rather than compile and review the official "Robin and Bruce's Approved List of Family Structures," suffice it to say that in our world, if you consider yourself a family, regardless of if we agree with your choices and beliefs, then you are a family. Period.

Okay, now that the whole "What defines a family?" question has been answered, we can move on to the sticky situation of the baby humanoids, often called "children."

We know that the topic of children can create all kinds of awkwardness and tension in a room. We collectively make assumptions about the role children play in people's lives, we assume people want or are planning for children, and we make people without children feel like outsiders in a world that has made children the ultimate destination of all people and the sole purpose and preoccupation of women.

So while this is a parenting book, we make no assumptions that everyone should be a parent, that everyone wants to be a parent, or that everyone is able to be a parent even if they yearn to be so. Becoming a parent or primary guardian of a child is not for everyone and must not be the measure of anyone's worth or value. If at any point we have communicated this idea or do so in the future, we apologize for being exactly what we hope our children are not—asshats.

But hold on there—not so fast. Not everyone is the primary parent in a child's life, but we all have children in our midst, from nieces and nephews to those rascally kids down the street to the child who merely crosses our path because of circumstances. Not having legal responsibility for a child does not mean you abdicate the collective responsibility we all have to care for and protect all children.

Now, before you get all carried away, this responsibility

does not mean that we can become those adults who offer unsolicited and passive-aggressive parenting advice to strangers at the grocery store—more on that later—but it does mean that we must take seriously the responsibility that we adult folks have in the lives of the children in our lives: in our families, in our neighborhoods, and around the world. Yes, in our understanding of the world, we are all charged to some extent with raising all the children of the world.

So about those children...

As we offer these ideas, we know that we have had a relatively easy go of it as parents. Our three daughters, so far, have not caused their parents huge amounts of pain, strife, or struggle. For this we are grateful. That said, we fully recognize that this is not the case for all parents and their children. We know from friends and families that how a child "turns out" is formed by many things—some circumstances we understand, and others we do not and cannot. Some children have physical, mental, or emotional realities that create great tension, conflict, and struggle because of how society perceives and responds to difference. Other children, because of things like family systems, class, gender, race, or geography, are impacted by the stark reality that has derailed and deconstructed the myth of "the American dream" or the idea that prosperity comes "if you just work hard enough."

With all of the variables that impact child-rearing these days, it is not enough to say that parenting is hard. The truth is that in such a complex and chaotic world, there are times when parenting will feel like you are being continually pelted by swirling debris that only comes from a physical, social, and emotional class 5 shitstorm.

While we very much commiserate about the parenting struggle and the yearning for effective parenting tips, tools, and strategies, we are in no way offering a foolproof cause-and-effect child-raising process, nor are we claiming to have have found the holy grail of parenting that is guaranteed to produce children of magnificent character, infallible values, and stunning achievement. If we thought that we had all of the answers or thought that some version of predefined perfection was the goal, we would have titled this book *How to Raise the Perfect Child*, or *If You Don't Raise Your Kids Like This, You Don't Really Love Them*, or *Screw the Village: We Know the Best Way to Raise Your Child*, or *How to Raise Kids Who Will Make Enough Money so that You Can Retire to Maui, Play Golf Every Day, and Greet Each Morning with an Acai Smoothie Sipped Through a Compostable Quinoa Straw*.

OK, at this point, you may be ready to toss this book into the recycling bin while screaming, "Well, thanks for nothing, Robin and Bruce! You've painted such a lovely picture of what it means to be a parent. Why should we even try? You suck! I hate you. No, seriously, I hate you."

Sorry about that. We just want to be honest about the ramifications of thinking that you are in control. Knowing you are not in control does not mean that how you parent and live as a human being is not important and has no impact on the children around us; it does—but "if this, then that" thinking works better for computer programming than parenting. It might be more realistic to say, "If this, then maybe that," or "If this, then hopefully that," or even "If this, quite possibly, if we have done the best we can and surrounded them with good people, and outside forces have smiled upon us—then that."

The kind of parenting that regards children as programmable machines that can, will, or want to mimic everything presented to them is highly subjective and is often an exercise in arrogance and privilege.

"Whoa, did they just mention 'privilege'? We thought this was a safe, hippie-talk-free book about parenting." Cool your jets, Sassy McSasserston, but yes, effective parenting today, especially in the United States, requires us all to understand the nature and impact of privilege.

Privilege has to do with race, class, socioeconomics, geography, and any time we associate a particular group of people or social location with the labels "good" or "bad" and assume that our experience is the norm. We see this played out when we praise parents whose children do well. We give all the credit to hard work and good parenting without ever acknowledging that some children simply have better resourced educational systems, more access to economic opportunities, in-place support for emotional and physical health emergencies, and enhanced opportunities for social exploration. There is never a guarantee of success, but some children are are given a head start and a better chance for success.

Privilege, and the false sense of superiority that it creates, can also impact how we view and react to children's achievements and struggles. When children from a certain demographic fail, there is a shocked sense of disbelief. People gasp, "But they came from such a good home," because good homes only produce children who burp sunshine and fart rainbows. Conversely, if we see children from another demographic behaving badly, we immediately blame the parents for not "raising them right," and children who do well from the same demographic did so despite the parenting at home—as if "those people" couldn't possibly be good parents. We essentially sit on our throne of privilege and cast aspersions upon those whom we perceive as different while giving a pass to those whom we deem normal.

And possibly the most insidious form of privilege is when we parents claim all the credit but fail to acknowledge that, in the United States, not all children are treated equally or have the same opportunities as other children. Race, gender, sexuality, economics, privatization, and other factors impact how our children are treated, educated, and influenced. To ignore these realities is to give children a false sense of self, either overinflated or dangerously low. Helping our children understand that there have been and always will be forces working both to help them succeed *and* to place obstacles in their way equips them to navigate the world with that much more wisdom, humility, and insight.

Again, all of this does not mean that parenting does not matter. After all, if we thought this was a total crapshoot, what the hell would we be doing writing this book? What we hope to convey is that this parenting thing and the children who have been gifted into our world are messy and will require of us the courage to see the work not as a burden but as a joyful (most of the time) opportunity to explore the complexities of life like no time before—and to help the next generation to be better for it.

With so much to acknowledge and navigate, we certainly have fought the urge to be overly directive in our children's lives. We have, for the most part, held a broad view of life and maintained some perspective on the impact and causation of our own actions. We understand that, when it comes to raising kids, we can do our best to provide an environment where they can thrive, and try to model what we hope to see—but parenting is still like consulting a Magic 8 Ball that continues to tell us, "Do your best and they will turn out fine." What we are attempting to do with the resource that you hold in your hands is to tilt that fortune-telling sphere a little more in your favor.

So if nothing else, please know that we offer these ideas with much humility, generous amounts of optimism, and a smidge of playfulness. And we do so in the hopes that you will find a few meaningful nuggets that will help with the particularities of your parenting journey.

SISTERS, 2007

Introduction to the 101

Don't worry—we are almost to the rules.

As you read through the rest of the #DontBeAnAsshat handbook, you will find is a list of 101 life lessons and life hacks. These are the most important lessons, morals, and tips that we hope to pass on to our children: Evelyn, Abby, and Analise. Some of these rules come second nature to us, others are aspirational, and still others are firmly planted in the "do as we say, not as we do" garden of good intentions.

But before we get to the list, there are a few things to know that will give the journey more depth and texture.

First, because Bruce is clearly the superior parental unit, he has done most of the writing. Jokes, people, jokes.

The reality is that Robin has one of those "real job" things where she is required to put in actual hours:

- In the same place
- Every day
- With people keeping track

For the past decade, Robin has been an instructor at a local community college, and she brings home the steady income that ensures that food, shelter, and health care make regular appearances. While Bruce's jobs are real too, most of his workday consists of sitting in coffee shops, riding in airplanes, speaking at conferences, and writing down words good. The overall writing breakdown is about 80/20, with each item on the list marked with a "Mom" if Robin wrote it and a "Dad" if Bruce did. We collaborated on most of the writings not in the list, but for the items in the list, depending on the topic, we have written in either the first or the second person.

You will notice that we have called each lesson a "rule," causing the rule followers to squeal with glee and the rule benders to break out into a cold sweat. We hate to disappoint either side of the aisle, but we chose "rules" as a format to normalize the list and stay within the "handbook" theme. Choose whatever metaphor you need to feel good about the list: guides, lessons, statutes, decrees, whatever—just make sure that you understand that each rule must be translated for the particularities of your parenting styles, the children in question, and any contextual variables. As we have said, you will get no easy answers from either of us, only insights and what we hope are helpful guides for the journey.

The list itself went through quite a view revisions. Beginning with well over a hundred suggestions, we whittled it down to the 101 items that we have included—and then we tweaked and shifted as we went through the writing process. In the process, we had to cross out, combine, and reword, but in the end, we agreed that each is part of our common parenting mindset even if we may approach each topic in different ways. In other words, even though we divided the 101 rules up between us, none fall into the category of "Only Robin thinks this is a good idea, but Bruce thinks it's totally whack!" You will also know we have not said this because Bruce rarely says "whack." Rarely.

We have written these rules and the "extra gravy" at the end of the book in the form of letters. We considered writing the book to parents in order to make our case for why each rule was important to pass on, but we found it more genuine to write as if we were addressing our own kids. Who knows—maybe someday one of our daughters, caught in a moment of indecision, will think to herself, "I wonder what Mom and Dad think about farting, having good sex, or making guacamole." Well, now she can just pick up this handbook and find out.

We feel strongly that it is important for our kids to be able to *do* as well as to *know*, so in this list we offer lessons that are both big-picture ideals and practical how-tos. Many of the lessons that we pass on to our children are not just about being a good person and caring for others, but also about surviving in the world as independent and functional humanoids. In other words, we try to offer a few tips for living so that our children can actually accomplish basic tasks without immediately calling a professional, paying a lot of money, or giving up without even trying.

At some point you will notice that this list is not laid out in a particularly organized structure. We contemplated using categories like "Household Tasks," or " Loving Your Neighbor," or "Don't Put That Up Your Nose," but we felt as if that would communicate an unrealistic image of the parenting pathway. This list is not organized into neat, compartmentalized categories because, let's face it, few things in life are linear in nature. Parenting is no exception. What we have done for the most part is give you situations as they may appear in your view—randomly and without notice.

Keeping in line with our commitment to practicality, you will also notice that the entries for the list are quite short, and there will surely be times when you will want more information. In these entries, we tried to find a middle ground between "death by lecture" and "because we said so" experience. Keeping these to roughly 250 words each was no small task. This length forced us to carefully craft our words and to be creative in how we expressed our ideas. What we gave up in not providing lengthy disclaimers, context, and extra details, we made up for in getting right to the point.

And before you call us out, yes, this list is full of contradictions: speak up *and* be silent, be determined *and* let things go, andbe polite *and* swear. These are a few rules that we try to hold in tension. Again, parenting, like life, is full of ambiguity. It might be easier if we parented in a social, cultural, or personality vacuum, but we don't. There are many variables that go into making parenting decisions in any situation, so we must all be able to adapt and change depending on the context.

We hope that we have offered a broad enough scope of responses in the final 101 that you will have plenty to choose from.

While we think it should go without saying, we are going to say it anyway: for the love of God, please do not take these lessons as some kind of recipe for raising the perfect, athletic, kind, world-changing hippie child—which, by the way, would be awesome, but would be an unfair expectation to place on any parent—because this is not a step-by-step instruction manual.

As we have said before, falling into a cause-and-effect parenting perspective is dangerous for a few reasons. First, it hardly ever works. Our actions and the responses of our children are simply not that clear or instantaneous. Second, it assumes that your child is impacted solely by outward influences and that your child's behavior has been shaped solely by something that the parents did or did not do. And third, if we believe that our kids act or don't act in a particular way solely because of what we have done, we fail to recognize that each child is different, with a unique personality, temperament, and set of instincts and developmental realities. So yes, you make an impact, a really, really, really important one, but there will always be a large amount of chance and circumstance that you have zero control over. We as parents must do our best to equip our kids with hearts and minds that can navigate these things and make good choices along the way.

We know that you will not agree with every part of this list and that you will have ideas of your own. In no way are we claiming that our 101 rules are exhaustive or that these are universally accepted parenting principles. If you plan on giving this resource to your own children—an excellent and officially endorsed parental decision—you should feel free to scrawl a big ol' "Aw, hells to the no!" in red marker across the rules that you think are idiotic. And if you think of rules that you hope to pass on, we have included a few blank pages where you can add your own. Have at it!

Finally, and most important, as you read this list of our parenting rules, we are relying on your ability to translate each one for the specifics of your family's structure, experience, and personality. Throughout this list we have woven in ideals that form and mold the heart, mind, and spirit. We are keenly aware that not each of these will work for everyone and that not every parent can exercise some of these things. In the end, no matter how much we may wish for consistent guidelines, each situation and the best response for it will vary. Exactly how these play out in the healthiest ways will depend on your ability to read and respond to the nuances of your own family dynamics and personal preferences.

There are no secrets to parenting. All we can do is treat the journey as a gift, tend to this gift as best we can, respond to the changes that will come, and love the entire time. Do those things, and no matter what your journey entails, you'll most likely be just fine.

OK, you have waited long enough.

Now on to the 101.

The 101

PHOTO BOOTH FUN, 2015

Rule #1: Make good choices (Dad)

About 15.69 percent of my parenting self wishes that I could control the world so that you would never have to confront difficulty, experience failure, or have your heart broken into a million tiny pieces and strewn about in a sea of despair.

Alas, if you lived in such a world, while you might be "safe" in the strictest sense of the word, your life would be lacking in texture and depth. You see, that other 84.31 percent believes that how you will grow as a person and become uniquely you is by venturing out into the world and experiencing heartache, jubilation, frustration, and accomplishment.

As you explore the world, it is our job to give you enough direction so that you will be equipped to, as your grandmother still says to her children and grandchildren, "Make good choices." Some directions will be familiar: "Don't light anything on fire, don't get arrested, and don't torment young children." Other directions are more broad: "Be kind, think of others, stand up for yourself, fall in love, be open to the possibilities, and don't forget your mom's birthday." Specific or general, all are meant to help you, yes, make good choices.

The guidance we offer changes as you and your parents mature, but our hope remains the same: that you go into the world, experience the breadth of wonder that exists within it, and thrive as a person in body, mind, and spirit.

So go, make good choices, take responsibility when your choices don't quite work out, and don't forget to call.

Rule #2: Don't be an asshat (Dad)

While I will undoubtedly have to make a substantial contribution to the family cuss cup for my generous use of the "A word," it's totally worth it. If you only remember a few lessons from this handbook, please make sure this is one of them. After all, I'm paying a lot of money to have it included.

There are a few things that make one decidedly *not* an asshat. Nonasshats know when to speak up and when to listen, value the experiences of others, and understand that kindness, compassion, humility, and thoughtfulness are essential traits as they go about life in their communities.

To be an asshat, however, is to believe that the world revolves around you, your needs, your whims, and your opinions—on all things. Asshats not only believe these things but freely let everyone else know. Asshats have something to say about *everything*, whether they have any knowledge of the topic or not. Asshats must have the last word. Every. Time. Asshats have little regard for the lives, feelings, or experiences of others, and when called on their asshattery, retreat into postures like, "You're being too sensitive," or "I'm just saying it like it is." And a big Asshat Alert is any statement that begins with the words, "I don't mean to be [sexist, racist, a jerk], but..." because asshats think that that disclaimer gives them a pass for saying things that are, in fact, sexist, racist, and jerky.

This book is our attempt at giving you every chance to avoid adding to the level of asshaterry in the world. Read it well.

Rule #3: Live with gratitude (Mom)

Gratitude rhymes with attitude — something you already know a lot about, my sweet children — and that is what it is, an attitude of gratefulness. Gratitude is no accident; it is an essential life skill to be gently cultivated through the years of your life. Ironically, those who seem to have the least to be thankful for are usually the best at gratitude. We can learn from them, as gratitude reminds us of what is truly important.

Right now I am grateful for:

- The homemade cinnamon rolls I ate this morning
- My three beloved daughters
- The strong but vulnerable man of great character I married
- My coat (it's cold outside)
- My students

Science agrees with me. Grateful people are generally happier; they have less stress and are better connected to their communities.[1] When you feel overwhelmed, when the ugliness of the world gets ahold of your heart, or when you want to give up, gratitude can be a balm for your soul and a source of strength, giving you the chance to recenter yourself, focus on what is truly important, and move from pain to healing.

For your mental, spiritual and physical well-being, even and especially when you are not feeling grateful, do your best to cultivate gratitude. Every. Single. Day.

---

[1] The John Templeton Foundation, "Infographic: What Good Is Gratitude?" November 20, 2013, https://www.templeton.org/grateful

Rule #4: Welcome the new kid (Dad)

Back when elementary school was K–6, in sixth grade I switched to a new school. Yep, I was the new kid.

I've never been a wallflower, but even so, I remember my relief when a couple of guys invited me to toss the football around during recess. At soccer, school, scouts, or church, being the newest person — unless you are one of those really outgoing people who thrives in these settings — sucks.

Many problems confront you when you're the new kid: people are judging, you are judging, new personalities surround you, you have no shared experiences to talk about, and relationships between others are naturally stronger. New folks, by the very nature of their newness, are starting at the bottom floor, whereas the rest of the group has had years of climbing the stairs together.

One of the kindest things you can do is to genuinely welcome new kids. This means that you should offer simple and subtle gestures of welcome: invite them to sit with the group, ask them about their interests, introduce them to your friends, and ask them if they need any help finding their classes. Not all folks will be ready to open up and tell you their life stories, but I can almost guarantee you that the gesture, whether or not it is visibly or audibly appreciated, makes a difference.

As hard as it might be to do the welcoming, you know that it's triply as hard to be the new kid hoping that some kind, any kind, of welcome is offered. Go welcome the new kid.

Rule #5: Ask for help (Dad)

In a world where self-reliance is lifted up, admitting you need help, asking for help, and accepting help are hard to do.

But dear, sweet independent ones, in your life you will need help. Be it in academics, athletics, work, or anywhere else, over time you must learn the best ways to seek and accept help.

In this case, I am not talking about help relating to work tasks, math problems, or soccer moves, but as it relates to your emotional and physical health. We live in a world where in times of distress, "taking one for the team," "toughing it out," and "sucking it up" are seen as positive attributes, and we are taught that seeking help is a sign of weakness. This life approach is not helpful because when you avoid or ignore genuine emotional and physical trauma, you risk things getting worse, not better.

When it comes to your body, don't risk a lifetime of injury and pain because going to the doctor is inconvenient or you don't want to appear weak. If the doctor clears you to play, fine, but remember: you're not a doctor, and even if you were, it's said that doctors make the worst patients.

When it comes to your emotional state of being, if you *ever* feel overwhelmed by life, please talk with someone. Do not let yourself get to the point of believing that there is nowhere to turn or that ending your own life is the only way to alleviate the pain and struggle. It's not. It. Is. Not.

In the end, listen to your body and listen to your soul, and when either cry out for help—ask for it.

Rule #6: Return the shopping cart (Dad)

Some people think that returning the shopping cart to the front of the store or to the collection area is a waste of time. They would rather leave it precariously sitting in between two cars, propped up over a cement boundary, or just haphazardly rolled into an empty space.

Returning your cart to the designated cart stable is only a waste of time if you don't care about who will follow you into that parking lot. By returning the carts, we help others to avoid dings on their cars, keep from taking up parking spaces with carts, and prevent a myriad of other accidents that could be caused by wild herds of shopping carts running rampant on a windy day.

A little extra effort and a small amount of time not only keep us from bringing about bad things but can also be a source of goodness for others. Imagine the relief that a store worker would have if they came out, ready to wander the parking lot in search of wayward carts, only to see them all in the place where they belong. I have also seen senior citizens arrive at the store to an empty cart area and have to rely on others to retrieve carts for them. Seriously, don't make your grandma go chase shopping carts in the parking lot.

Applied too to such acts as refilling the ice tray, clearing your dishes, or replacing the toilet paper, thinking of those who will follow and responding with care instills a little kindness into the world, and maybe others will pass it along.

Rule #7: Share your parents (Mom)

Your dad and I have a strong belief in the importance of living in community. This means that sometimes we will loan you out to other trusted adults. Experiencing other parenting or leadership styles and being cared for in different settings is good for you. This also means that sometimes your parents will give attention to other children, maybe your friends or maybe kids you don't even like. In order to create a stronger community for you, your parents may need to:

- Coach an elementary soccer team
- Volunteer in your classroom
- Schedule a bazillion cookie booths
- Organize parents of middle school athletes
- Go to boring meetings
- Hand out Band-Aids, tissues, or encouragement
- Bake persimmon cupcakes
- Lead tours of your school

Ironically, even though we do this for you, sometimes you will resent it. In a way, I suppose you are right to resent it because we don't just do it for you. We do it—when we are able—for the good of the community, just as you benefit from the community that provides you with teachers, coaches, scout leaders, and other parent leaders when you need them. Sometimes that kid you don't like much might need us more than you do at that moment. Sharing your parents graciously is the gift you give to the community.

Rule #8: Don't tell other people's stories (Dad)

We are a family of storytellers.

Like knights at the round table, when we gather as a family we regale ourselves with tales of epic adventures, embarrassing family moments, and touching remembrances of relatives who have paved the way. Without fail there are the stories that we *always* tell about one another, there are the stories that we wish would be struck from the family lexicon, and there is *never ever* any embellishment, revisionism, or hyperbole. Never.

Generally our storytelling is good-natured and helps to build up our already resolute family relationships. That is, until someone tells a story or shares something that was not theirs to tell or share. Sometimes we unknowingly embarrass a child or share a conflict that the other party was not ready for the entire clan to know about. We often do this unintentionally, but at other times we are simply behaving passive-aggressively—not that I have *ever* done either of these things.

What is important to understand is that not all stories are yours to share. Each person's level of privacy is different; some people are not comfortable with having relationship conflicts adjudicated by the entire family, and some people would prefer to tell their own embarrassing stories.

In the end, err on the side of restraint. Tell the stories that make you look like a jackass or a social misfit, but when it comes to other people—let them tell their own stories.

Rule #9: Make guacamole (Dad)

What can I say—people love your dad's guacamole.

Over the years, you have seen me make it, but what you don't know is why. I make this dip for two reasons: First, it's important to have a popular go-to dish that you can bring to parties and one that you can prepare in your sleep. Second, my go-to dishes are ones that I like—also my spinach dip and chicken adobo—so accidental leftovers or a last-minute party cancellation mean guacamole for dinner! We all win.

Dad's Guacamole Recipe, *a.k.a., Big Bowl of Green Goodness*

Directions: In a large bowl, mash all ingredients, and devour.

- 6–8 avocados (pitted* and scooped)
- 3–4 roma tomatoes (diced and drained)
- 1 medium red onion (finely diced)
- 2–3 cloves of garlic (peeled, crushed, to taste)
- 1 jalapeño (roasted, seeded, diced, to taste)
- 1–2 lemons (juiced, seeded, to taste)
- 1–2 limes (juiced, seeded, to taste)
- 1 bunch of cilantro (chopped)
- 1 cucumber (peeled, seeded, and diced)
- Salt and pepper (to taste)
- Shredded sharp cheddar cheese (sprinkled on top)

*To keep the guac from turning brown over time, keep 2–3 pits in the bowl during storage. Don't know why it works, but it does.

Please feel free to play with this recipe to make it your own, but even more important, find your go-to and go for it.

Rule #10: Taste everything once (Dad)

One of my greatest pet peeves is not picky eaters in general but picky eaters who choose to dislike something without ever having tasted it.

Sure, there can be good reasons for people to avoid certain foods without first trying them. If there are genuine aversions to smells, allergy issues, or dietary restrictions, then yes, please do avoid things that will make you barf, swell up, or raise your blood pressure. No problem there.

We are under no delusions that everyone will like every dish that is placed before them, but in our home, you are not allowed to hate it until you taste it. I kind of feel the same way about movies, art forms, and my jokes, with the point being: how will you discover new things unless you try—at least once?

What this means is that you must fight through initial feelings of revolt, aversion, or fear in order to discover things that might expand your world and bring new colors, tastes, and textures to your taste buds. Sure, you will occasionally get a "What the hell was that?!" experience, and not every food will become your favorite dish, but I dare say that more times than not, you will discover that there is a reason that many foods have been passed down from generation to generation—they feed the stomach and nourish the soul.

So yes, this is mainly advice about food, but be it a new place to visit, a new skill to learn, or a new food to eat—before you decide that it is not for you, give it a try.

Rule #11: Wait tables (Dad)

Working in the service or retail industry changes how you treat people. It's far too easy to drink the nectar of condescension, causing you to believe that you could do other people's jobs better when you have never done them before.

I waited tables and tended bar for many years during college and graduate school, and it was by far one of the most transformative experiences of my life. I met interesting people from all walks of life, I was humbled by the how hard the work was and that my grandfather had done this until he was in his seventies, and I experienced firsthand how many people treat "servants" with disrespect, arrogance, and condescension.

It's important for everyone to work in some industry where they work with clients, the public, or customers because it changes the lens through which we see and then how we act.

- **Tipping:** You'll tip better because you know that tipping is a way that many businesses get away with not paying well and servers get taxed on tips, received or not.
- **Efficiency:** As a customer, I no longer assume incompetence and inefficiency. I trust others have thought these things though better than I have.
- **Servants:** Yes, servers provide a service, but they are not servants to be disrespected and treated as slaves.

There are many jobs that have the same effect—airline gate agents, teachers (especially any of mine)—and doing any of these jobs will make you a better person for it.

Rule #12: Use credit wisely (Mom)

There are times, like when you're buying a house or a car, when debt allows you to do things that would otherwise be impossible. Sometimes debt can be a good thing. But debt can easily become a tyrant, limiting future freedom with a lifetime of payments toward something that was used up long ago.

Compared to other times in history, credit is easy to get today. Sadly, it's a common practice for credit card companies to target students who may not yet be savvy about credit. Before long, people in their twenties get buried by consumer debt and loan payments that they may never emerge from.[2]

Many families are uncomfortable talking about money, which doesn't help you kids. Your dad and I have personally experienced the huge negative impacts of taking on more debt than we should have. Yes, you will have to build your credit history, and borrowing is sometimes a good idea. But question, strongly question, any purchase that makes you use credit for more than a month. Do you really *need* it? Do you really need it *now*? Will you be able to pay back what you owe *for the entire term of the loan*? Will the long-term good outweigh the loss of spending freedom during repayment?

Using credit is a serious obligation, and being indebted to big business can be a heavy burden to bear. Remember: "Where your treasure is, there will your heart be also." (Luke 12:34 NRSV)

---

[2] Jeff Grabmeier, Credit Card Debt: Younger People Borrow More Heavily…" *Ohio State University Research News*, January 14, 2013, http://researchnews.osu.edu/archive/creditrepayment.htm.

Rule #13: Say you're sorry (Dad)

It is one thing to say, "I'm sorry," but quite another thing to mean it in a way that will change your future actions.

As you grow older, not only will you be able to remember times when I apologized for my behavior, but also you will have seen that I tried to change. Whether I lost my temper, made assumptions about what you were thinking, or unfairly compared you to another sister, I hope you know that, when I have apologized, it was not just to address my regret but also to let you know that I would try to be better in the future. That said, apologizing is hard to do.

I hope that you find ways to know when you need to apologize, and then do it. Some perceive apologizing as an admission of imperfection and thus a sign of weakness. What I hope you know is that being able to apologize is a sign of strength, precisely because you are willing to admit that you are not perfect. While apologies are difficult and humbling, you will find that, when accompanied by a change in behavior, they make relationships stronger.

As wonderful as you are, you will mess up. With coworkers, family, friends, and even strangers, you will do and say things that will make a negative impact. When these things occur, you will be challenged to decide if you are willing to make things right with an apology and a commitment to change.

I trust these things will not happen with regularity, but when they do, please have the courage to apologize.

Rule #14: Forgive others (Dad)

If holding grudges were an Olympic sport, the Reyes family would be draped in medals. Your Grandpa Reyes was one of the kindest and most forgiving people I have ever known, and your Grandma Reyes was loving in her own way—but forgiving others was not one of her strengths. And yes, this grudge-holding gene has been passed down from generation to generation, and your dad and Lola ("Grandmother" in Tagalog) have it bad. I also get it from my Chow side, so yeah, you're welcome.

I have been accused of being overly understanding, even naive, when it comes to the foibles of others. There may be some overcompensating, because I also know that my grudge holding has led to the end of friendships and has damaged relationships. I've worked on being forgiving over the years, but as I reflect on the many names still carved in stone on my list, I am reminded how unforgiving I can be.

I implore you to do your best to break the cycle of such intense grudge holding and forgive people. Forgiveness does not mean that you simply forget or allow yourself to be taken advantage of, but it does mean that you give up some of the weight of grudges and resentment. When you do this, you may see that others can change, relationships can be strengthened, and you can be changed for the better along the way.

Seriously, it can happen—you just need to be willing to forgive others and believe that they can change.

Rule #15: Pick up the poop (Dad)

Someday, should child-rearing be part of your life, you too will have a child *cough* Abby *cough* who decides that the topic of her fourth-grade persuasive writing project will be, "Why we should get a dog." When this happens, you will bargain, make agreements, and yes, probably find yourself with a new canine curled up on the couch before you know it.

When we got Fawn—full name Farrah FAWNcett—you girls agreed to pick up the poop, walk the dog, and so on. Well, let's be honest, you have not picked up as much poop as you all promised, and the only walks the dogs get these days are from the bed to the couch. Good thing Fawn and Vespa are so cute. Guess we'll keep them despite the long con you have pulled off.

Of course, we played our part as well. While it would be great if nine-, eleven-, and fifteen-year-olds would always be responsible, this is probably not a fair expectation. We also haven't reminded you to pick up the poop as much as we should have. Our bad.

The lesson is this: when you make an agreement, do your best to honor what you have agreed to. Sometimes this requires you to hold strong and demand that another party follow through or else break off the relationship. At other times, you will need to be flexible and shift expectations. Also, like kids and dogs, when you know that there is a high chance that one of you may not follow through, you need to be OK with that.

Oh…and if you're free, the dogs need a walk.

Rule #16: Ignore what other people think (Dad)

There will be times when you know that people are talking about you. Gossiping, making assumptions, spreading lies, or just plain talking shit are to a certain degree always part of human gatherings. You must rise above it because, at the end of the day, you cannot control or predict what other people are going to think, say, or believe about you.

Plain and simple, this sucks.

When these things happen, you will feel hurt, betrayed, angry, and disillusioned. Friendships will be tested, and you will be left wondering, "Why?" There is not much that we can say that will alleviate these natural feelings, only that in the midst of these situations, you must do your best to not let the despair and disappointment overwhelm you.

But we won't leave you with "Just don't worry about it" as our counsel. Here is what you can do: tell folks in whatever way possible, through others or directly, "If you want the truth, just ask me." It is an unhealthy use of your time and energy to attempt to chase down and correct every rumor that may or may not be circulating out there, but healing can happen when others are mature enough to come to you directly.

We are sorry that these things have happened and will happen. To know that you will be hurt by what other people think or say about you brings us deep sadness. We also know that you can rise above it, live out the confidence of spirit that dwells deep within you, and be the you that we know you are.

Rule #17: Listen to what some people say (Dad)

An important skill in life is to be able to know which voices should be listened to and which ones need to be ignored. While you must certainly ignore those voices intended to tear you down as a person, there will be voices that will also speak to you in the hopes that you will be built up.

These voices are not always easy to pick out. There will always be the obvious: mentors, trusted friends, family members, and your greatest foam-finger-waving supporters, Mom and Dad—but voices of encouragement and wisdom may also come from unexpected sources. Be open to the wisdom of strangers, suggestions from colleagues, and new perspectives from the next generation—for you never know when something that you say, produce, or share may spark a reaction in another person. Sometimes that spark will be wonderful and full of affirmation, and at other times it will generate challenges and passionate disagreement, but often, when you handle those well, it will help you grow in more ways that you can imagine.

While we don't want you to define yourself solely based on other people's expectations, assessments, and opinions, being open to input is an important skill to learn if you are going to grow emotionally, socially, and professionally. So yes, ignore that which is meant to tear you down, but also embrace the voices who are leading you toward being a better person.

So basically, you be you—with feedback.

Rule #18: Pay the cuss cup (Dad)

You have grown up with a cuss cup.

Some of you have been a bit rigid in the policing of language in our home—I still maintain that "crap" is not a curse word—and for the most part we are grateful that "potty-mouth" is a word that folks generally don't use to describe you.

That said, swearing can be an effective means of expression. With a few words of guidance, you have our permission, blessing, and encouragement to drop the occasional bleep-worthy comment, rant, or reaction.

- Like screaming, swearing is a perfectly understandable and acceptable means of expelling pain and stress, especially after a painful stub, bump, or burn.

- Like violence and sex in movies, gratuitous swearing lessens the impact, but a well-timed and intoned F-bomb can communicate a thousand ideas.

- When it comes to dropping the F-bomb on the idiot who cut you off and can hear you: I can guarantee you that telling someone to do something to themselves that is anatomically impossible will only make things worse.

- If you are not sure about the crowd, just use any of the following euphemisms: "Shut the front door," "Cheese and rice," or "Mother trucker." All get the point across.

So yes, swear as you need, be liberated in your expression, and be nuanced in your usage. In doing so, you will find a freedom that few other things can provide. Eff yeah!

Rule #19: Shop wisely (Dad)

Mom talked about using credit wisely, so I get the shopping entry, because, well, I'm the shopper in the family.

We all view money differently. Some folks sock it all away, and it takes them a huge amount of effort to spend it on anything, while the phrase "burning a hole in their pocket" is far too applicable for other people. Never spending beyond your means is a given, but when you do shop, here are few things to remember and consider so that you can spend your ducats well.

Compare. In today's online world, there is no excuse not to comparison shop. Taking into consideration shipping, urgency, and budget, take the time to find the best deal.

What is your time worth? Unless you are shopping in order to be part of the crowd, think about when you should go shopping in order to save time and frustration.

Red tags. Whether you're shopping for clothes, groceries, or travel, always be on the lookout for the clearance prices and clearance prices on top of clearance prices.

Want versus need. *Wanting* something and *needing* something are not always mutually exclusive, but knowing the difference between the two can help you make better choices.

Pause. Now, I admit, this has taken me a long time to grasp, but in a world of instant gratification, pausing before you buy can only help you make better spending decisions.

Finally, if you are going shopping anytime soon, that Father's Day motorcycle is definitely a *need.* :-)

Rule #20: Ride the bus (Mom)

My generation is leaving your generation with a world in extreme environmental distress. This sucks, and it's one of the ways I have failed to even scratch the surface of my intentions.

One of the most effective ways to combat environmental degradation is to increase the use of public transportation, especially in the United States. The world cannot support one car per person, and we must all let go of that "ideal."

Not only does riding the bus allow you to see neighborhoods and communities that you wouldn't otherwise, it also does away with the stress of buying gas, finding parking, or worrying about parking tickets. Riding the bus also has benefits beyond environmental virtue or financial frugality. The bus gives you the freedom to go out on your own before you can drive, so you can be more independent and take more initiative for your own time.

Riding the bus also develops your radar during a time in your life when there are people close by to help. You will occasionally encounter a creepy individual on the bus, and we want you to trust your instincts and keep yourself safe. Because you will also spend much riding time with people who are of different educational, social, and/or aromatic classes than we are, you also must learn that these people are not creepy and not dangerous, just different. Riding the bus keeps us humble, helps us stay grounded, and makes the earth smile.

Don't miss your stop!

Add your own...

_____

_____

_____

_____

_____

_____

_____

_____

_____

_____

_____

_____

Rule #21: Look up (Dad)

Every once in a while, it's important to look up. Not only could you be the one who warns the world of a stealthy alien zombie attack—seriously, why does no one ever look up in the movies?—but when you look up, you see the world differently.

No, this is not a rant about the evils of walking around with your face buried in your phone—though paying attention while you are walking is always a good idea—but about the practice of seeing more than what is right in front of you.

As you observe the world, walking down the street, sitting with friends at a cafe, or simply being outdoors in the nature, seek things out that are not obvious. Look up, look to the sides, look behind you, and even look behind that thing that is right in front of you. Linger a bit and seek out the nuances of your surroundings, notice the unnoticeable, and absorb the texture and depth that your view provides.

It's easy to see what the world wants you to see in people and relationships, in society and culture, and in politics and systems—so looking beyond the easy view makes them all fuller and more complete. When you do this, you will be able to notice those who live on the fringes by choice or circumstance, you will see emerging ways of thinking, and you will simply have a more complete version of the world in which you live.

So look up at, linger upon, and embrace the beautifully complex world that lies before you—and yes, please watch where you are walking.

Rule #22: Don't make others late (Dad)

Sometimes I can be a bit uptight, rigid even, about time. What I have come to accept is that we all see, treat, and experience time differently. And. That. Is. OK. Still, as flexible and chill as I have become, some advice:

Don't create time crises for others. One of my favorite quotes is, "A lack of preparation on your part does not constitute an emergency on mine." Asking for help is fine, but don't become that person who is always asking in a frenzied panic for others to bail them out at the last minute. Don't stifle your creativity, but if that creativity is experienced as a disregard for those around you, you will quickly find yourself on your own.

Honor the time others have carved out. There are people in my life who are always late. I usually roll with it, but generally I think consistent tardiness is disrespectful. If someone has made time for you, honor that gift by being on time or at least letting them know if you are running behind.

Appreciate how others experience time. Intellectually I understand that not everyone operates with the same internal timekeeper. Of course truly appreciating that fact is a daily struggle. But I've learned my own rigidity can be unproductive, and I've had to let go of my assumptions about time in order to see a world that moves forward at different paces. And ultimately that is the most important thing.

So don't be rigid about time and timeliness, but live in ways that honor others and the time that we have.

Rule #23: Pack with purpose (Dad)

Packing is an art. OK, that may be a little over the top, but learning to pack well—your car, luggage, cabinets, or refrigerator—can save you much time and frustration in life. I learned from the best, my stepdad and your lolo (Tagalog for "grandfather"). These packing lessons did not come easily. There were tears, many late nights, and much cursing. So you're welcome for passing on this art of packing minus the struggle.

Visualize the space. The most important thing you must do is estimate whether or not you will be able to fit everything that needs to fit. It may take a few failures before you develop the ability to gauge the space, but in time you will become a pro at this. Folks watching will say, "No way," but like a mighty wizard, you will prove them wrong time and time again.

Make a pile. Until you have mastered visualization, before you start packing, put everything in a pile. This will avoid surprise items that will throw off your packing progressions.

Pack tightly like Tetris. Start with the larger items and fill in the gaps with the smaller items that can help support and cushion. Be firm, but don't break stuff. Like in the video game Tetris, empty space will be your downfall.

Unpack for the next time. After a long trip, it is tempting to just throw everything into storage. If you take the time to unpack well, folding, cleaning, and drying everything, your stuff will be easily packed the next time.

Thus ends your lesson on the art of packing.

Rule #24: Finish the task (Dad)

There will be moments in your life when, in the midst of a project, you'll just want to scrap it all. Term papers, work projects, relationships, or personal goals—sometimes the crap gets so thick that the only option seems to be to push yourself back from the table and go see a movie. The crap will change —it will be people, circumstances, or your own actions—but it will be there, and you have to figure out how to deal with it.

While there are certainly times when walking away is your healthiest option, there are also times when you just gotta plow through and finish the job. It's not always easy to know when, but just know that difficulty does not always translate into "not worth your time," and here is why.

Finishing honors and values others. Sometimes you will have no choice, but failure to finish a task can damage and devalue relationships and commitments that others have made.

Finishing honors and values self. When you make a promise to yourself, do your best to honor it. This means being realistic, but it also means being persistent and committed.

Life's steps build one on another. There is no guaranteed linear progression of life, but often completion of one task creates opportunities for taking on future ones.

Beauty is often on the other side of conflict. You will be amazed at what is on the other side of hard work, tension, and struggle. Finish enough of the time to find out.

Finished.

Rule #25: Let things fail (Dad)

As important as it is to honor your commitments, there are going to be times when you must simply walk away, leave things incomplete, or allow things to fail.

Knowing when it is time to push through and finish and when it is time to let go and walk away is a dance—a dance that that lasts a lifetime. Holding on too long to tasks, relationships, and situations creates complicated webs of unhealthy dependence. Walking away too soon creates spaces of unresolved conflict and anxiety.

There is no way to know if it's time to let something fail, but here are a few questions to ask as you are deciding.

Is there any joy? Sometimes we must deal with difficulty and obstacles. And while the tough stuff can be fun, if you feel as though you are losing life, it may be time to walk away—no success is worth your health in body, mind, and spirit.

Has it become about you? Often we are afraid if we leave, everything will fall apart. For any long-term project, this means that things have become more about you than the project. Yes, be vital, but avoid becoming irreplaceable.

Is death being delayed? Too often we have difficulty letting projects die. Endings can be done with dignity and care, but before we can see birth, we must first welcome death.

Rarely will walking away "feel good," but even in the midst of any doubt, guilt, or grief, know that it is often out of failure that our greatest successes find their beginnings.

Rule #26: Tip the housecleaners (Dad)

Whenever we stay at a hotel, when we check out, we always leave a thank-you note and some cash.

In an ideal world, people would make wages that were livable and would not have to rely on tips. Unlike in some countries where tipping is purely a reflection of a job well done, in the United States, many employers assume that service workers get tips, so they pay less overall. We tip hotel workers in particular because many hotels simply do not pay living wages. Also, working in hotels is so physically taxing that many employees end up hurt, so tipping is a way to offset lower wages *and* to send a message of solidarity with the workers.

Other people we encourage you to remember to tip, because they rely on your generosity and commitment:

Restaurant workers. In seminary I worked as a food server and bartender, and they are taxed on assumed tips.

Curbside baggage handlers. You can often handle your own bag, but if you are able to, let someone help anyway.

Shuttle drivers. Again, you can probably handle your bags, but giving a few bucks to the driver is a good thing to do.

And the rest. There are so many jobs that rely on tips, so please also tip folks like your manicurist, hairstylist, barista, cab driver, valet, and anyone else who provides a service.

How much you tip can vary (10–20 percent), but I hope that, even if the service is less than stellar, you will still tip. You never know how your gesture may impact that worker for good.

Rule #27: Speak up (Mom)

Through example and experience, women are often taught it is safer to stay silent. The same goes for young people and people of color in this country. You are all three—female, young, and brown—but even if you weren't, I would encourage you to gather your thoughts, find your voice, and speak up.

No one can be a better advocate for you than you. In this world, few things are given without your asking. Many more things will be given if you ask for them. As a teacher, I experience this every day. Students who ask for help will receive it, while those who need it but stay silent may only get it if I notice and have time. It is an unfair but true part of life. You may have to be persistent and insistent, but don't be afraid to voice your opinions or to ask for what you need.

Sometimes you have to speak up to protect your rights and opportunities or they will be taken from you. Not only do you need to speak up for yourself, you should speak up for others who aren't being heard. Be a voice for the voiceless and excluded and for those whose voices are discounted or ignored.

Speaking up is not without its risks. Malala Yousafzai survived an attempt on her life for speaking up for education, and Harvey Milk spoke up for gay rights and was assassinated. You have to be brave to speak up because you will face rejection, jeers, judgment, anger, and retribution. But when the moment comes, don't be afraid to lift up your voice and speak.

Rule #28: Carve the turkey (Dad)

As you all know, in our home, at age thirteen, you get to (have to) carve the Thanksgiving turkey. The beautifully browned, bacon-drenched bird is placed before you; we hand you the carving tools; and after a little coaching, you dive in.

We hope that you see this as more than a silly thing that Dad has you do and that you embrace this rite of passage as an acknowledgment that you are growing up—and that we trust you with knives. :-)

Other family rituals and rites of passage that we pass on:

Owning a phone. When you were in sixth grade, or had to take the public bus home, we gave you a phone. All that we asked was that you texted us when you left and arrived.

Going to the mall. This also includes concerts, boba, and anywhere else you went on your own with friends and without parents. When we allowed you to do this was less about age and more about our trust in you to be responsible and respectful in public.

Having a debit card. Again, different times for each of you, but when we felt that you could handle having money at your fingertips (money you earned), we allowed you to use a debit card to help you see how you used your money.

We do not take any of these things lightly. These passages are a way that we say to you, "We trust you, and we are letting go," and a way for you to claim your agency, live into your personhood, and experience life on your own terms.

Rule #29: Do things without being asked (Mom)

If I came home one day and found that the living room had been cleaned, the dishes done, the laundry sorted, and the floor vacuumed, I would be stupefied with wonder at what magic had enchanted my house.

This is magic within your grasp.

Seeing a need you can meet and then meeting it without being asked or expecting attention for it is a sign of character. It shows that you observe your world, not just for what you can get from it or how it can entertain you but for how you can improve it and help others around you. This is often very simple. For example, you can:

- Pick up trash that's not yours.
- Help a teacher carry something.
- Offer a seat to an elder in a crowded room.
- Bring dinner to a grieving friend.
- Close a locker left open.
- Call your grandparents just to say hi.
- See rule #15.
- Do any of the chores listed in the first sentence.

Doing things without being asked shows initiative. Instead of waiting to be told what to do, you can jump in with a solution. Many people won't ask for help but appreciate it when it's offered. Don't wait to be asked; work this magic whenever you have the opportunity. You never know; your one kindness may inspire many, many more.

Rule #30: Tend to your friendships (Dad)

Maintaining friendships is hard work.

There are always those people you can connect with after years apart and just pick up where you left off, but most of our friendships require a little more time and care. Friendship is not just about the amount of time but about how that time is used and valued. Specifics will change depending on the person, but here are a few ways to tend to your friendships.

Use social media. Mark your friends (and family) on your social networks as important, so you receive notifications when they post a picture, tweet, or update. You don't always have to respond, but make room in your internet life to make sure you're up-to-date with life's happenings, magnificent or minute.

Send a note. Electronically or on one of those paper things called notecards, take time to share your journey, to ask what they are up to, and/or to simply check in about life.

Grab coffee. Yes, this could also be lunch, boba, or a beer, but whatever the cuisine, take the time to schedule and follow through on spending some time with your friends.

Remind them of your friendship. In every conversation I have with my friends, there is always a moment to express my support, encouragement, or empathy. Reinforce the relationship by living the best parts of what friendships can be.

Again, tending friendships takes time, but as we live through the joys and our sorrows of life, nothing is as meaningful or as vital to our lives as true friendship.

Rule #31: Cherish your siblings (Mom)

Not everyone is fortunate enough to have siblings, but I believe they are an irreplaceable treasure. For most of us, siblings are our closest companions through life's early years. We don't always get along, but siblings are our first lifelong partners. Siblings have a common generational perspective on family experiences; we are survivors together. This does not mean they are always like us; indeed, siblings are often the first point to our counterpoint. But like it or not, your siblings are part of the foundation upon which you will build your life.

Even if you only see each other occasionally, there is something special about someone who has been with you all along. Even when you're not getting along, siblings know you in ways other people never will. For example, no one else would remember the game of Spider & Hand that my brother, Brian, invented to entertain me when I was little, not even my mom or dad. It saddens me immensely that your uncle died before you ever really got a chance to know him. He was a special brother. Even if we hadn't spoken in a while, I knew I could count on him. And I wish that for all of you with each other.

Girls, you shared a household for many years, you survived life with your crazy parents, and someday you will likely have the shared duty of taking care of us. My hope for you is that you communicate as often as you can, see each other as often as you can, and help and cherish each other as well as you can—as accomplices in the journey of life.

Rule #32: Trust your gut (Dad)

Call it intuition, a nagging feeling, or the Holy Spirit—sometimes you will simply need to trust the voice whispering from your soul and act.

It would be great if, every time you had to decide something, your gut would be banging a bass drum or holding up a neon sign to let you know that you were on the right track. Unfortunately, more often than not, it is the subtle whisper from somewhere deep inside you that is your best guide, and it's not always obvious.

When I am confronted with a situation and feel conflicted about what to do, I usually know the right decision. My initial reaction and internal voice may be subtle, but they do speak. Sometimes I listen. I also know that, despite knowing better, I can be influenced by outside forces: wanting to please others, worrying about image, or not being willing to deal with the inconvenience that the right choice will cause.

That inside voice does not just come out of a vacuum. It is there because we have surrounded you with people and experiences that have developed an internal guide for you. This voice will need tending; it needs to be fed, and it needs to be nurtured. Because like your outside self, your inner self will change as you grow, and so too will the whispers guiding you along the way.

Trust your gut. It is a lifelong journey to nurture and trust our inner voices—but one that is vital to living a life of meaning.

Rule #33: Sing loudly (Dad)

Few things are more humbling than sitting in a cafe and realizing that you are singing out loud while wearing earbuds.

As you know, the only thing slightly more mortifying is being stuck in the car with me while I am dropping some smooth rhymes along with Run DMC or showing off my pop vocal skillz with a little Adele—and doing those things loudly.

I hate to break it to you, but while embarrassing your teenagery souls brings me a wee bit of joy, I sing loudly in the car even when you are not around. I know that you already sing loudly all the time, and I hope that you never lose the ability to bust into song and do so at the top of your lungs.

It is cathartic. I am sure there is some science behind it, but being able to sing and sing loudly just feels good. Even the worst day, crappy situation, or random bad mood can be tempered with a few lines of the Taylor Swift song of the day.

It keeps you humble. Unless you are making your living with your voice so have good reason not to occasionally roar with song, please never think you are too cool or too old to sing and sing loudly. You will never be too old or too cool.

It reminds you of your past. The songs I love the most are the ones that remind me of where I have been. Songs remind me of past love, fun moments with friends, meaningful life experiences, and world events. Music stirs the soul, so you might as well stir with the volume dialed up to MAX.

All right, so who's DJing? It's time to sing!

Rule #34: Fall in love (Dad)

Falling in love is awesome—love gives texture to life, gives depth to our emotions, and opens us up to the possibilities that can unfold before us in body, mind, and soul.

I have never been one of those dads who feels like he has to protect you from interested romantic suitors. In fact, I hope you fall in love. That said, here are a few things to remember as you fall in and out of and back in love again.

Love allows the other to grow. Crucial to healthy love is that you and the person you love grow together *and* that you allow one another to grow into the person you are supposed to become. You will not always agree on politics, faith, food, or family, but it is a gift to find joy in how the other grows, even in different ways, and still be able to find connection and cohesion.

Love requires working through conflict. It often seems easier to avoid talking about tough issues in a relationship. Over time, however, conflict causes resentment to fester and eventually be expressed in unhealthy and destructive ways. When you feel resentment start to build, be brave and talk.

Love sometimes means walking away. There may be times in your life when, for the sake of your mental, spiritual, and physical health, walking away is the right thing to do. This is never easy, but if you ever find yourself in any kind of abusive or destructive relationship, please walk away.

While we are in no big hurry to see you fall in love, when it does happen, know that, we are rejoicing for you.

Rule #35: Hang a picture (Dad)

Everyone should possess basic household skills, like being able to hang a picture. Being handy gives you a sense of accomplishment, saves you money, and with the right guidance, keeps you from ending up with a wall full of holes where hooks were mounted incorrectly—or so I've heard.

To hang a picture well:

- Find the "stud," a.k.a., the wood behind the wall, and put the nail or screw there.
- If there's no stud, a wall anchor keeps a screw securely mounted.
- Use a level to make sure things are even and level—don't try to eyeball everything.

A few others tasks that you should know how to do:

Mow the lawn. Assuming that you have a yard, learn to trim a shrub, mow the lawn, and plant flowers. Embrace nature, get your hands dirty, and take care of the yard.

Plunge the toilet. Look in the tank to see how the mysterious flushy thing works. One day, you'll have to replace it. And when plunging a clogged toilet, to avoid splatter, be gentle.

Don't electrocute yourself. When it comes to electrical stuff, outsource. Pocked walls can be patched, and floating poop can be cleaned up, but bad electrical work can kill.

And above all, don't afraid to ask for help and give it a try. After all, only by being prepared, trying things, and learning each time will you make that hook eventually stay in the wall.

Rule #36: Assume goodness in others (Dad)

There are those in the world who walk around in fear: fear of what people will do, fear of what people will steal, fear of how people will act toward them. Because of past experiences, some have good reason to be ultracautious, but I believe that the world has also succumbed to the idea that our initial reaction to others should be fear.

That is no way to live.

As you go through life, I hope that you'll do so without the assumption that every other human being is trying to get one over on you. There is enough pessimism and distrust in the world that you need not add to it. In fact, what the world needs are more people who believe the best about people when others cannot, who see potential in people when others have given up, and who allow people to be in the world without having to prove they are worthy of being treated with dignity.

I am not saying to be foolish, let yourself be taken advantage of, or remain in unhealthy relationships; I only ask that you give being generous of spirit a chance. Sometimes you will be taken advantage of or be let down, but for those whom you allow dignity, you will do immense amounts of good. Some people are distrusted at every turn of the corner, bear the weight of undeserved assumptions, and rarely receive goodness; you relieve a small amount of that weight with gestures that assume dignity, humanity, and hope.

And that is a good way to live.

Rule #37: Watch your drink (Dad)

At some point, you will drink booze. And not to give permission, but your mom and I also know that you may drink before you reach the legal age. These are choices that you will have to make, and unlike your dad, we trust you will be wise. That said, here are a few tips when it comes to drinking.

Be brave. Some people drink to be brave, but in this case, I hope that you will be brave in in your relationship with drinking. Don't drive after drinking, help those who have had too much, and model wisdom in your libationary practices. Do not give in to unhealthy pressures.

Drink water with your wine. Hangovers are often brought on by dehydration, so always drink lots of water even if it means a drink in both hands. This goes triple on sunny days!

Watch your drinks. In no way do we want to place the blame or responsibility on you for jackasses who may try to slip drugs into your drink, but you do need to be aware that there are jackasses who may try to slip drugs into your drink. Always watch your drink and your friends' drinks, and if you are ever in doubt, play it safe and toss them out!

Avoid alcoholism. If you ever feel that your drinking is impacting your life in unhealthy ways, or someone near to you raises concerns about your drinking, know that there is a family history with alcoholism—not widespread, but it's there.

So there you go. Enjoy your beer, wine, or fancy booze like your grandmother's—but be wise about it.

Rule #38: Don't flip off the truck driver (Mom)

Once upon a time there was a young woman who drove through an intersection. She found herself being followed by a tow-truck driver who clearly thought she had not properly waited her turn at the intersection. The truck was large; her car was small. The driver was large; she was not. The driver honked and yelled at her as he drove behind her. Angered by his reaction, she made a poor choice and, well, gave him the finger.

Turns out, it was not the right gift for this situation. He then followed her, still yelling and honking. At one point, she stopped her car, thinking that perhaps she should try to talk to the driver. He stopped his truck, ran over to her car, and started pounding on the window and yelling. She drove away, and he still followed. His driving and behavior were increasingly threatening, and she had long since regretted her rash action. In the end, she did not drive home as she was intending but drove to the closest police station and stopped in front. The driver finally drove off at that point.

The lesson: don't let your anger bring you to do stupid, harmful, or dangerous things. I'm not saying anger should be bottled up but instead that you should let your anger stutter so you can express it in a way that doesn't cause unnecessary damage. Anger begets anger, over and over, so consider the outcome of your actions. Channel that anger into something productive instead.

And yes, the brash, middle-finger-waving woman: Mom.

Rule #39: Learn your history (Mom)

You come from a rich and varied cultural heritage that I hope you continue to understand and appreciate more deeply throughout your life.

So much, both good and bad, has brought about the world you know, and understanding how we got where we are is key to moving forward. Knowing the struggles that have made possible the many opportunities you enjoy in your life is an essential part of never taking anything for granted. Knowing about the utter evil that humans have done to each other is key to recognizing and fighting evil wherever you may encounter it.

Women didn't gain the right to vote in this country until my grandmother was twelve years old. I'm sure this was part of why my she was always careful to vote in every election. Knowing generations of women to whom this right was denied helped her value it for the precious opportunity it is. Until 1936, women who married Asian immigrants lost their American citizenship and often became citizens of nowhere. Your mom and dad couldn't have legally married in California prior to 1948. Your great-grandfather (Dad's side) was involved in strikes in the fight for farmworker rights, but your great-great-grandfather (my side) was likely a member of the KKK.

We must learn from the good and the bad in our history. You need to know all of this to really understand how precious the opportunities you have are and to accept your duty to work for a more just society.

Rule #40: Give back (Dad)

There are few character traits that we hope you will live out more than gratitude and generosity.

Generations upon generations before us have generously sacrificed so much to pave the way for us. We hope that remembering those who gave so much of themselves will not produce feeling of guilt and obligation but rather a thankful and generous spirit. We hope you will see that giving back to the community is how you can say thanks to those who gave before and how you can prepare the way for generations to come.

And while there will be times in your life when giving back will seem more or less convenient, more or less impactful, and more or less important, we hope that you will give.

Your money. Whatever your financial state, we hope you will support causes that align with your passions, people who are doing amazing things, and strangers who may need help.

Your time. Presence can be a gift. Sometimes an hour once a week, or a monthly visit have more impact on an organization or individual than any amount of money you can give.

Your skills. At some point, you will discover gifts and skills that can help others. Being generous with your talents will allow others to better utilize their own.

Giving back can often feel overwhelming, but as we have discovered over time, when you give back, you will also be gifted with experiences and insights beyond your imagination.

Add your own...

_____

_____

_____

_____

_____

_____

_____

_____

_____

_____

Rule #41: Kiss your lola (Dad)

One of the things that you just learn about in our family is greeting people: how to greet someone, whom to greet, and in what order you must greet them.

When you arrive at a family gathering, there are many unwritten and important rules:

- Give hugs and kisses on the cheek.
- Be sure to acknowledge everyone who is family.
- Greet any new visitors as if they were family.
- You go to those who are older.
- Those who are younger come to you.

I am not sure that we ever instructed you on the etiquette and rituals, but somehow you absorbed the nuances of the greeting dance, and they have become part of your DNA. Some of this is certainly cultural, stemming from both your Chinese and your Filipino roots, but there is also something universal that you can learn from how you greet your family in a room.

Not only are you paying respect to generations who have come before you but you are also reminded that there are generations who will follow you—and in both we hope that you find comfort in the fact that that you are part of a community. On more than one occasion, we have had to explain if the person you just kissed was your auntie or uncle by blood, church, or neighborhood. It is in this expanded community, we also hope that your understanding of family broadened and lived.

Who is in the room? Your family.

Rule #42: Have faith (Dad)

You were born into a faith tradition.

We have chosen not to give you a free-for-all faith experience but rather to ground you in the faith into which you were born: the Christian, Reformed, Presbyterian variety. At some point you will question our faith choices, you will question the beliefs we have taught you, and you will search for a faith that feeds your soul. That may end up being the faith of your birth or it may be a different tradition.

Wherever you end up on your spiritual journey, we hope and encourage searching and seeking. We understand that you have agency and freedom, but as you discover you beliefs, we do have our hopes about any faith that you choose. Let it be a:

- Faith that informs your politics and civic life
- Faith that builds relationships beyond the circles of your own comfort and circumstance
- Faith that empowers you to grow into who you are intended to become professionally and personally
- Faith that values empathy, compassion, and justice
- Faith that invites questions
- Faith that you can lean on in times of despair
- Faith that claims something stronger than any human acts of division, violence, or destruction

Where you will land in faith we do not know, but we hope you will land in a place where your soul will be fed, your mind stretched, and your heart made full.

Rule #43: Protest (Dad)

There will times when you must publicly protest.

There will be whispers and shouts from all around you telling you not to go out into the streets, not to give voice to your righteous indignation, or not to join with others in expressing outrage at injustice. The tactics that you may use will vary: marches, sit-ins, civil disobedience, et cetera. Still, there will be times to lend your ear, listen for the call, and decide.

We hope that when you hear the call to public protest you will answer it. Be wise in your actions, but know that for generations, change has been sparked by those who are courageous enough to step out of their comfortable situations and join with others to demand justice, compassion, and peace.

The issues or events calling you will also vary. Sometimes they will directly impact you, sometimes your friends, and sometimes strangers. You will be challenged to make hard choices about loyalties and tactics. People will tell you to play it safe or to remain calm. There will be times to step back and think more systematically, but there will also be times to walk the streets, join hands in solidarity, and even risk harm.

We in no way wish for you to foolishly put yourself in harm's way, but we do want you to know that there will be times in your life when you should be bold, walk for justice, and protest that which must be called out—and when you feel that call to the streets, we hope you will take the step and march.

Rule #44: Giggle like a middle schooler (Dad)

If I had a dollar for every time your mother said to me with a touch of exasperation, "You are such a middle-school boy!" I would have approximately $1,478.

Sure, sometimes it may happen at the most inopportune time, over seemingly innocuous words like "balls."

"Inaugural balls." *giggle*

"Put your balls away." *giggle*

"Who left the blue balls on the floor?" *giggle*

So yeah, middle schooler, right here—guilty as charged.

Thing is, sometimes in life we forget how to play, notice whimsy, and just be silly. I hope you never get to the point where you are unable to find playfulness in the things around you, no matter how "mature" and grown-up you are supposed to be.

Yes, be appropriate—though the child who whispered "balls" to me during communion at church obviously missed that class—but also allow yourself to be silly. For when we allow ourselves to loosen up a bit and drop some of pressure to be focused and productive at all times, we can actually become more focused and productive because silliness changes us.

So be silly, giggle at juvenile things, and allow yourself to exhale, breathe, and take a break. When you are able to do this well, you will, in fact, be able to be a better grown-up.

Oh, and one more thing: balls.

Rule #45: Never lie to your doctor (Mom)

I've read several articles recently about how often we lie, something like eleven to fifteen times a week. Even those of us who greatly value and pursue honesty—we too falter. However, as I have often repeated to you children—cue conspiratorial eye rolls behind my back—there are three people you should never lie to: your doctor, your lawyer, and yourself.

Most of the time I follow that up with something like, "...and if you do, you are stupid." My children know well how sweet and sensitive I am. You see, it is not in your best interest to lie to someone who must have the absolute truth in order to help you. For instance, if I lie to my doctor about how much I drink, it means my doctor doesn't have all the info needed to diagnose me or prescribe medication. My idealized self could end up causing serious damage to my well-being.

Telling the truth to my doctor or lawyer requires that I first be honest with myself, brutally honest. This is the crux of the difficulty. If I allow myself to equivocate in evaluating my own behavior, I don't have to admit it to anyone else, and I don't have to take responsibility for it. If I ate too much, drank too much, spent too much, hurt someone, or did something else I regret—admitting the negative things that I did takes courage. Having the courage to admit that we are who we are, owning up to our warts, is sometimes the hardest thing to do—but, it is also the first step toward becoming the honest embodiment of that ideal we wish to be.

Rule #46: Don't mock (Dad)

Teasing has always been a part of our family.

It's easy to cross, sometimes unintentionally, that line that moves you from good-natured teasing to mocking. Playful teasing done in a spirit of community is one thing, but mocking that tears at the very nature of a person by belittling something about them is quite another thing.

Mocking becomes unhelpful when it makes someone feel inadequate, disrespected, or somehow stripped of their humanity. This don't-mock policy has many applications.

- When a food server drops a tray of stuff, don't clap.
- When a friend doesn't understand something that everyone else does, don't make them feel worse by focusing on their lack of understanding.
- When someone picks at your or a friend's physical or social insecurities, don't do that back to them—despite how good it might feel.

Some may say that we are asking you to be overly sensitive and that you can't control how others feel. That may be partially true, but even so, we would hope that you err on the side of not being hurtful or belittling. Remember: words have the power to make people feel bad about themselves.

Being measured and being careful with your words in light of how they might impact the soul of another takes effort and work, but wouldn't you want the same care taken when others think of you? I hope so.

Rule #47: Talk about the sex (Mom)

Ahhh, the sex. Whether or not I chose to talk to you about it, you would learn about it, and given how ubiquitous it is in TV and movies, surely sooner than I did. Sex is important and can bring great emotional and physical joy or pain. It is a basic human need and is at least as important as pooping, and in the early years, we talked to you a lot about that.

So let's talk about sex—again.

I have thought it was important for us to talk about sex, too, in age-appropriate ways. I started when you were young when you asked questions about where babies came from. Despite my own initial discomfort, I've actually used the words "sex," "penis," "vagina," and "breasts" with you—Although we are not above using euphemisms for comedic effect. Balls!—so by the time you hit puberty and the discussions became more important, we already had some shared context.

"Must we talk about this again?" Yes, before you can read that last Twilight novel. Yes, before you go to high school. Yes, after you get your period. Yes, after almost any TV show or movie. Because society has exposed you to so many unhealthy examples of sexual relationships, I want you to develop an understanding of what is healthy or unhealthy. I want you to understand contraception so you can choose when you want to have a baby, and I want you to avoid HIV and other STDs.

I want sex to be a source of joy to your life and your spirit, and for you to gain understanding, we must talk about it.

Rule #48: Have good sex (Dad)

Yep, sex advice from your dad? Not. Awkward. At. All.

Never fear, no diagrams or visual aids will be used. But since Mom chickened out about writing this section, you get Dad's thoughts on sex. Like I said: Not. Awkward. At. All.

As you develop intimate relationships (of which sex will be a part), you will discover positive and negative ways in which you view all facets of a relationship. Sex is no different than the other aspects, so because I hope that you will have a healthy understanding of your sexuality—here are a few pointers.

Be connected. Be sure that you have some emotional connection with your partner. This is not about the duration of a relationship but about how the most intimate of physical acts is enhanced when there is a deep and genuine emotional bond.

Be free to explore. You should not feel confined or coerced in your sexual life. With mutuality, you and your partner should allow one another to explore your sexual relationship without feeling physically forced or emotionally pressured into anything that is not comfortable to you both.

Be communicative. Neither you nor your partners are mind readers, so to avoid building resentment, you must talk about sex: needs, hopes, expectations, and joys. While it can be difficult and uncomfortable, talking is vital to a good sex life.

OK, you can turn the page now—or move on to the fart lesson if that will break the awkward bubble that you have been in for past few moments. End. Of. Awkwardness.

Rule #49: Be a good leader (Dad)

At some point in your life, through calling, coincidence, or circumstance, you will be asked to lead. This may mean something grand like leading a group of people working toward a common cause, or it may be leading a small project with people who need someone to help them accomplish a task. I hope you will, at some point, answer the call to leadership.

Leadership is not just telling people what to do and expecting them to do it. Sure, some treat leadership like that, but I don't believe that that is good leadership. Good leadership helps a group of people have ownership over their destination and shows the leader's willingness to do their part in helping the group get there. Your job as a leader is to do the following:

Listen to the people you lead so they are heard but also so they play a part in building all aspects of the journey.

Act on what you hear to in order to make hard decisions, challenge people to succeed, and better know your role.

Release others to take on tasks and responsibility in areas where they have interest, passion, and competency.

Reflect often in order to discern what may be holding you back from achieving the goals you have set.

Adapt leadership strategies, perspectives, and practices in order to stay contextually appropriate and effective.

In the end, the most important aspect of leadership is care for the people you are leading. If you have that, they will know, and when it's communicated well, they will follow.

Rule #50: Be a good follower (Dad)

I have been what many consider a leader in a variety of contexts. I know what it's like when folks who are part of the group I am trying to lead are less than helpful. I am sure that I have made my share of mistakes, but I also know that, in a culture where we often focus only on leading, we have devalued the importance of being able to be follow.

Make no mistake: being led is not easy, but knowing when that is your role in a particular time or project is vital to the success and health of any group or community you are part of.

Here are a few tips on how to be a good follower.

Ask for clear expectations. In relation to the end result or to specific tasks, to lessen confusion be sure you know what is expected of you, your group, and even the leader.

Do what you have agreed to do. Nothing is worse than taking on a task and not completing it. People count on you, and when people trust you to do something, follow through.

Voice disagreement and affirmation. If you only voice disagreement, you will eventually be ignored. You might be right, but if you're being ignored, you can't make an impact.

Do not undermine or be divisive. No matter how frustrating a situation might be, be upfront but honest, or even leave, but don't participate in or reinforce destructive behavior.

I have no doubt that you will have many opportunities to lead groups of people. I am just as sure that you will be that much better of a leader if you have been a better follower.

Rule #51: Find your people (Mom)

I recently had lunch with a good friend whom I don't see often. As we discussed life and politics, we came to the agreement that, "Life is so beautiful. Life is so shitty." And it is. To help you make the most of beauty and survive adversity, you need to seek out and embrace the kind of community that feeds your soul; you need to find *your* people.

Your people are the ones who know you by name and always invite you in. They might tease you mercilessly, but underneath the jokes, there is always love. They are the ones who inspire you, who push you to be better or to try new things. Your people will tell you the truth, even when you don't want to hear it. They might be your family, your soccer team buddies, your college squad, your church, your neighbors, or even an online collection of kindred spirits.

Humans are social animals; for most of our history, we existed in tribes. I'm not saying it is bad to be an introvert— introverts are fabulous—but I am saying sustained isolation isn't healthy. I believe that to truly thrive we need community, and each of us needs a support system that is comfortable and familiar, yet bigger than ourselves. True community is a living force, sustaining us even as we help sustain it.

When you find your people, you will have help discovering life's beauty and company to appreciate it. You will have hands to ease your burden and loving arms to hold you and inspire you with renewed hope and strength for tomorrow.

Rule #52: Be self-reflective (Dad)

There will be a moment in your life when you think you know it all. I am not just talking about book knowledge or work skills but the idea that you have reached some kind of completion of who you are as a person.

Fight the urge to think you are done growing and keep looking at how you can improve who you are. Yes, you are a unique person, a joy to your parents, and surely a good friend to many, but—I hate to break it to you—you are not perfect. There will always be areas of your life where you can improve: emotional health, relationships, management, and avocations, so embrace them and work on them whenever you can.

The resources you use to do this will vary, so be open to the ways in which others can help. Meet with trusted mentors, tend to your spiritual health, and seek professional help when needed. I also hope you use aids like the Myers-Briggs Personality Type indicator, Enneagram, and other proven tools to help in your introspection. However you engage in this discipline, be intentional about using tools that will challenge, inspire, and support you in your ongoing journey of life.

Some will say that admitting that you need to learn and improve is a sign of fear and weakness, but know that for many others, it is a sign of confidence and strength. Being able to admit that there are things to learn and then doing so is a strength that the world needs more of, so keep reflecting, keep seeking, and keep learning.

Rule #53: Clap when they can't hear you (Dad)

I love when you all react to movies.

We all know that Evelyn has the "most likely to react exactly as the director hopes the audience will react" award, but at one time or another, you have all been so drawn into a movie that you have clapped for a performance on the screen. The spontaneous applause was usually followed by trying to play it off and looking around as if you were not the one who clapped, but we all knew that you did it.

There is something telling about your spirit when you applause even when the intended recipient can't hear you. What you are doing is surrendering yourself to the creative storytelling of another person and allowing yourself to enter new worlds and new contexts. This is a beautiful thing to behold.

As you get older and more calcified in your understanding of the world (happens to us all), this will be more and more difficult to do. Just like you exercise a muscle that has to be worked in order to grow, exercise your openness to the possibility that someone can draw you a narrative and communicate an unfamiliar story to you.

This is not just about the movies either. This kind of openness is needed in all aspects of life and relationships. A willingness to absorb and applaud another person's creative expressions that touch your soul, spark your imagination, and move you to applaud, even in a darkened movie theater—this is a gift and one that will keep on giving.

Rule #54: Never lose hope (Dad)

The worst future that I can imagine for the world is that all hope would be lost. No, check that. The worst thing that I can imagine is that you, my daughters, would lose hope. Yes, some accuse me of being too idealistic, too optimistic, even naive. Thing is, I think people believe that being hopeful means sitting on your butt with your eyes squeezed shut, hoping that when you open them, you'll be kissed by rainbow-farting unicorns. The hope that I yearn for you to have is quite the opposite; it's the kind of hope that is grounded in seeing, knowing, and experiencing kindness, healing, and justice in the world. When you forget, here are few reasons to stay hopeful.

People love you. Believe this in your bones. It is true.

People do amazing things. Out of the great depths of their own pain, suffering, and injustice, people exhibit hope, kindness, and beauty. Never lose sight of those stories.

People are generally kind. Most people don't do newsworthy acts of love, but I have no doubt that most people are kinder on a daily basis than we ever give them credit for.

People overcome injustice. Rarely fast enough and hardly ever without great sacrifice, throughout history many have overcome injustice and persevered through suffering.

If you do feel like there is no hope, please do your best not to give in to the despair. In those times, reach out—to us, to your community, to a professional, to someone—because you, our child, are a great source of hope for others.

Rule #55: Remember others (Dad)

You may want to sit down for this. OK, here it goes: "You, my dear sweet child, you are not the center of the universe." Take a minute. It will be OK.

Your actions and words impact others around you. From how you conduct yourself at the wheel of a car to how you respond to injustice in the world, you have the capacity to help or hinder every day. Remembering others is not only about standing up for what you believe but is also about rejecting the idea that you live in some kind of social, cultural, or physical vacuum where there are no ramifications for what you do or say.

When you drive. Please avoid doing three-point turns in congested areas; don't double-park on narrow streets; and for the love of god, lay off the horn, or at least wait a few seconds.

When you walk. Don't block the sidewalk when you walk and faster walkers want to pass. And don't walk and text.

Following the rules. Some rules are made to be broken, but some rules have been made for following. Just because you don't understand or agree with a rule doesn't mean that it shouldn't be followed.

Feeling the disconnect. Apathy leads us to believe that most things are OK or that our actions are too distant to matter. When we fall into this trap, we reinforce unjust systems.

At the end of the day, just be aware that while you are special and unique and loved, so are the other people around you; just as you do, they also deserve to be remembered.

Rule #56: Play board games (Mom)

I hate board games; I don't know why, but I do. That said, I still believe you should play them. Together. As a family. Often...OK, maybe not often, but at least sometimes.

There is something wonderful that happens when a family gathers together to play a board game. Unusual alliances occur, children can vanquish parents, people learn cooperation and strategy, and we spend time together in a place apart from our everyday activities and to-do lists.

Other benefits include:

- Learning to take turns
- Enjoying the fun of winning
- Experiencing the challenge of being a good loser
- Discovering the power of thinking ahead
- Seeing that your actions have consequences
- Practicing making tough decisions

Communication during board games does not have a particular purpose other than to carry the game forward, which opens up an important space. I have learned more about what is going on at school during a board game than by repeated iterations of "How was school today?"

Perhaps more important, board games create a shared family language and experience and allow for much silliness, something we could probably all use more of. Where else would your dad have the chance to make so many bad jokes about sheep, wheat, and ore?

Rule #57: Look homeless people in the eye (Mom)

We owe each other respect just because we are all members of the human family. When you see someone who is homeless, whether or not they are asking for help, whether or not you decide to give them money or buy them a meal, you owe it to them to look them in the eye and acknowledge them as fellow human beings.

I have spent a significant part of my work life working directly with folks living on the financial margins of society, and even so, I know I have no idea how hard it is to get by without a place to call home. Just daily survival demands immense strength, perseverance, and character.

When you are homeless, people treat you worse than they would a dog. People make huge assumptions about you and your life. People yell at you and call you names, and you are often not even allowed to sit on the sidewalk and rest. Most people walk right by you as if you weren't there. Homelessness reminds us that bad things happen to people all the time, and it makes us feel uncomfortable. So we would rather ignore people and their poverty. It is easier to walk right by.

My children, you and I, as members of the human family, must do everything we can to communicate dignity to all people, especially to those who have had it stripped away on a daily basis. When you see a homeless person, shake their hand, ask their name, and look them in the eye.

Rule #58: Be cute, strong, and smart (Dad)

There will always be people who will try to put you in a box of "shoulds"—what you should do, what you should look like, how you should act, and what you should believe. Not all people are trying to oppress you, but they live in a confined understanding of whom they believe can and ought to be Asian American, female, Christian, San Franciscan, mixed race, educated, et cetera, et cetera.

We all do this kind of boxing in, as we can only understand the world to the extent that we are willing to be open to it, and not all people are able, willing, or convinced that seeing the broader world is a good idea. They will come at you with justifications, social pressures, guilt, and shame, but in the end, they want you to fulfill a particular cultural script, and no deviation is allowed.

So what we want you to do is be you. When you were little girls, folks would comment about how "cute" you were. And while we certainly thought you were adorable, we would follow it up with "and strong and smart." We did this not only to provide commentary on the way girls are often treated but also because we do believe that you can be all of these things if you choose to. You can be be a fashionista who loves soccer and math, you can be a math geek who likes frilly things and tree climbing, or you can be a geocacher who loves bath bombs and can burp the alphabet.

In the end: You. Be. You. Cute, smart, and strong.

Rule #59: Be adventurous (Dad)

A few years back, I made you go watch Roller Derby. We had no connection to Roller Derby, and no one had ever shown any interest in it. However, I had always wanted to check it out, and your mom and I hardly ever pass up an opportunity to have you experience the power that is kick-ass women.

So we went, and we soaked in the culture and the vibe. We ate hipster cupcakes and bought stickers, and you got to meet one of the skaters. And while we chose not to sit in the section called the Suicide Zone, it was pretty thrilling.

And then we went home, and we have not been back to see another Roller Derby since then. We tried it; we ventured into a new space, a space that we had zero context or knowledge of; and we simply lived that night.

There will be many forces telling you to remain where you are, be grateful for the life you have now, and avoid taking any risks. And while there are certainly times to be careful and deliberate, please do not be so cautious that you miss out on the adventures that may be beckoning from near or far.

I hope that, in your long life, you will take many adventures: experience different parts of the world, meet people whose passions will stretch your mind, and try new activities that will expand your experience of living. As you do so, be open to finding new passions in your own life and simply experiencing the adventure for the moment that it is.

Now, go.

Rule #60: Forge your own path (Mom)

In life, you must make your own way. Despite what you may think, your parents realize you are you, and not your siblings—even though we get your names wrong sometimes; sorry about that. Instead of feeling like you have to do what your parents or siblings have done, it is important to take time to explore what resonates with you, what you love to do, and what you get excited about. I hope that your dad and I have done a worthy job of encouraging you in this self-discovery.

The flip side of this is not being afraid to claim something as your own even if it was also done by your elders. I struggled with this in high school because I was really interested in theater, but Uncle Brian had basically been Mr. Drama just a few years before. I decided to pursue it anyway, claiming it and making it mine in a way that was different from how my brother did it.

Perhaps an even greater challenge in making your own way is when that way diverges from that of your friends. When your friends want to do something you know is wrong, it takes inner strength and some self-confidence to not go along. Or if your group of friends want to do something that isn't interesting to you, have the hutzpah to kindly say, "No, thank you," and then pursue what you are interested in.

Hold on to your strength of character and strike out on your own when need be. In the words of my middle child, "You do you, boo. You. Do. You."

Add your own...

_____

_____

_____

_____

_____

_____

_____

_____

_____

_____

_____

_____

Rule #61: Read for fun (Dad)

Not really sure that I am writing this rule. Full disclosure: this one goes in the "do as I say and not as I do" file, as your mother is much better than I am at this—much better.

Reading for fun is important, and I hope that over the years I will get better at this. I've gone through ebbs and flows in my fun reading, and honestly, you already all do it better than I do. Not only does reading for fun break up your academic or professional reading but long-form reading combats the trend of our attention spans growing shorter than a goldfish's.

You've already begun developing your own tastes, but when I'm in a good reading vibe, I like to read:

Murder mysteries. Any book where a murder is solved within a couple of days of couch-potato reading is my kind of book: murder, suspense, romance, twists, and turns. Bring it on!

Biographies. I love a good biography, especially about people I know little about. I find knowing a fuller version of any one person makes me appreciate and look for the fuller and more complete versions of everyone.

Historical fiction. Surprisingly, my favorite genre is any story that brings to life a different time and place in history. Done well, the writing paints the historical setting in a way that gives depth and texture to any story.

You'll have to ask your mom about her reading preferences, but just know that reading for fun is a habit we both hope you will hold on to for a lifetime.

Rule #62: Watch baseball (Dad)

Baseball is beauty: the double-play, hitting the cut-off, the history, the hit-and-run, the high heater, the numbers, the nachos—simply beautiful. And here are my ten reasons why:

Pitcher. Any shape or size can play: chubby, skinny, short, or tall—all are welcome on the field of dreams.

Catcher. Baseball is a team sport. In order to be successful, all twenty-five players must play their part.

1B. In a no-hitter, with a well-timed grand slam or diving catch to end the game, one person can make a difference.

2B. Every team has that person who can play multiple positions; utility and flexibility will keep you playing for years.

3B. With 162 games, the baseball season is a marathon requiring great mental, physical, and emotional discipline.

SS. From signs to timing a pitcher's delivery to backing up on every play, baseball is full of subtleties and nuance.

LF. Math nerds rule in baseball. Yes, there is "gut" too, but in the statistics, passion and planning are found.

CF. With the Angels, the Padres, and the Rays, who dropped "Devil" from their name, Jesus would choose baseball.

RF. The movies are awesome: *A League of Their Own*, *Bull Durham*, *For Love of the Game*, *Major League*, and so on.

DH. Suicide squeeze, Triple Crown, perfect game, frozen rope—this is more beauty than one species deserves.

And in case you were wondering, there is no pressure to be an Oakland A's fan for life. I will still love you-ish.

Rule #63: Be political (Mom)

You must be political in this life.

We humans are part of a worldwide community governed by diverse political systems, and an attempt to avoid politics has all the effect of the proverbial ostrich hiding its head in the sand. The world, and the politics that govern it, will go on without you. You don't get to choose to opt out of this reality. Not being political has a political effect, and guess what, your not being political is just what the wealthy powers want.

You have a role, and you have a unique voice, and you owe it to the world to express those. What do you want your school, your city, or your country to stand for? What are the core values you embrace, and are they reflected in the day-to-day procedures around you? If you see things you know aren't right, how can you make them better?

Don't confuse politics with the demagoguery (look it up!) that is happening right now in the political arena. People using fear and prejudice to take power is all the more reason for you to be involved in what happens to your world.

You also have a duty to speak for those who have no voice. Unfortunately, they number many in our current political environment. Seek out the young, the poor, the homeless, the disenfranchised, the excluded, and the targets of prejudice, and hear what they have to say. We need their voices just as we need yours to create a truly just world where everyone's humanity is valued.

Rule #64: Hold babies and attend funerals (Dad)

Without busting out into a chorus of "The Circle of Life" from *The Lion King*, we hope that you will have a healthy understanding of the rhythms of life, from birth to death.

Let's start with death. We don't want you to be afraid of death; in fact, we hope you will learn to embrace the reality of death as a natural part of life. We have exposed you to the complexities of grieving when someone has died, you have been forced to face the realities of violence after your uncle was shot and killed, and we have always placed value upon the death of pets in your life, going as far as storing your deceased pet rats in the freezer for months until we could schedule a proper burial. Being able to handle the emotional and spiritual processes of death and grief is vital to your growth as a human being because you will be faced with death through your life, and we hope you can hold the care and tenderness it demands.

Babies remind us of life in all its wonder, fragility, and complexity. While new humans are generally sturdier than they look, when we hold a baby, smell that baby smell, or listen to the cooing and the crying, we are reminded that life is a gift. And with that spirit, we are compelled to live our lives not only for our own survival but for the good of the world in which we walk and breathe.

At birth and in death we are reminded that life is precious and powerful. So as you go about your day and for as long as you live, live a life worthy of the gift of life that you have.

Rule #65: Scream as needed (Dad)

Every once in a while you will want to scream at the sky. Be it in anger, frustration, or jubilation, a good scream at the universe can be cathartic and good for the soul.

Scream out loud; scream out proud.

This may be a strange lesson to read because we are not really a screaming family. I am sure there have been times where you have wanted to—me too, but we have chosen sarcasm, silent stewing, and passive-aggressiveness as our modes of operation.

Again, you are welcome. ;-)

So yeah, while it's not a big part of how we raised you, scream when you need to: when an election goes terribly wrong, when someone breaks your heart, or when your parents get in the way of you living your life as you hoped to. Screaming can release pent-up energy, it can act as a release valve for anger, and sometimes it just feels damn good.

If at all possible, as you scream, be sure to choose your location well. You don't want to wake your neighbor's baby, startle your drill-wielding dentist, or give the person standing in front of you in line in the grocery store a heart attack—but then again, sometimes you just can't help it.

And finally, when it comes to screaming, when it comes from such a deep place of pain that you cannot hold it on your own, allow others into your world, so they can bear some of the weight of your pain—and in many ways scream with you.

Rule #66: Watch silly movies (Dad)

Yes, "silly" means different things to different people, but in this case, I am unapologetically talking about films that have the potential to make you giggle like a middle schooler.

I am sure that you will not watch most of these, but I hope that, on occasion, you will suspend the need for movies that inspire, move, or compel and allow yourself to simply laugh at poop jokes, giggle at sexual innuendo, and squirm when characters find themselves in awkward situations. I firmly feel that unguarded and unfiltered laughter is good for the soul.

In no particular order, a sampling for your consideration:

- *Spaceballs*
- *There's Something About Mary*
- *Blazing Saddles*
- *Zoolander*
- *Galaxy Quest*
- *So I Married an Axe Murderer*
- *Life of Brian*
- *Dodgeball*
- *Monty Python and the Holy Grail*
- *Wedding Crashers*
- *Airplane*
- *Nacho Libre*
- *Bridesmaids*

And I leave you with this wisdom from *Life of Brian*: "Blessed are the cheesemakers."

Rule #67: You do you online (Dad)

It must be weird growing up with a dad who actually does know about technology, social media, and the interwebs. And while there are things that you will just instinctively "get" because of your generational worldview, because of my work, I can offer a few words of internet guidance.

Pause before posting. Not only can you make sure all typos are corrected but you can also decide if the tone and content are really what you want to express. You can express anything online, but remember that there are ramifications.

Own your words. You will violate rule #1 and will offend someone. Don't be defensive or try to dismiss reactions. Just apologize. Also, don't delete your tweets. That's weak.

Don't overshare. Online postings are not your inside voice, the car, or your home, so what you say in private should differ from what you would say in public. If you wouldn't say it in a public space, it's probably best not to post it online.

Be fully-ish you. "Oversharing" is relative. Share your life to the extent that you are comfortable, but keep in mind that what you share can reflect on and impact those close to you.

At the end of the day, the internet is just a delivery mechanism, albeit an important and powerful one. It can be used to both build up and tear down individuals, communities, and relationships. It is my hope that the way you interact, share, and engage will offer a positive contribution to the world online and in person, just as you should offer in real life.

Rule #68: Spend time alone (Dad)

It is funny that I am the one talking about being alone, as few would say that being alone is one of my natural gifts. Truth is, as I have gotten older *harumph* *harumph* *harumph* I feel an increased need for quiet alone time. Not just because I think it's good for me but because I genuinely yearn for it.

There are many reasons why it's important to be alone. In fact, when you don't feel like you need it or when you don't want it, that's probably when you probably need it the most.

When you do find time to be alone, here are some tips:

Be still. Be comfortable and allow yourself to focus on your breath, your heartbeat, and your thoughts. This will help you to let go of some of life's noise and center yourself.

Be bored. In a world where we are constantly entertained and occupied, it takes great commitment to not always be moving. Feeling as if there is nothing to do allows us to discover new ideas, free of the weight of immediacy.

Recharge. While people's needs in terms of duration and setting vary, alone time allows us all to recharge. We need time to get distance from a conflict, time to focus on one project, and time to catch up on sleep. Time alone re-creates and reenergizes us in body, mind, and spirit.

Regardless of whether you think you need it or how long this time should be, we all need time to be alone. Please carve out some time from your schedule and commit to some alone time. Heck, if I can do it, you surely can as well.

Rule #69: Remember your immigrant roots (Dad)

Other than First Nations peoples, everyone in North America has an immigration story. Some people's stories began when their ancestors left their homes for religious freedom and exploration, some people were ripped from their homeland and brought to North America as slaves, and the immigration stories of others are unfolding with every arrival.

Everyone has a story, and it is important that you remember yours. We hope you remember and embody the stories that have been told over and over again: the sacrifices made, the discrimination faced, and the community experienced. And, of course, never forget the laughter, love, generosity, and feasting—all part of your story and ours.

Because there will always be newcomers and immigrants entering the United States, you must never forget our family's immigrant story. For by remembering our family's story, you will be able to better understand theirs. When we forget what generations before us did in order to create a life in the United States for us today, we lose empathy, forgo compassion, and create obstacles for people who are simply trying to do the same thing that our own family did generations before. Never forget.

Remember where you are from so much so that you treat those who are arriving today as if they too are worthy of the opportunities given to you. You are, and they are too.

Rule #70: Confront injustice (Dad)

We know you have seen it. You have experienced it. You may have participated in it. In school, on the street, and in your family, you have seen people being treated unjustly. In the face of our world's injustices, we must each decide what to do.

Our hope is that you will do something.

Showing up in words, actions, and attitudes, you will face injustice throughout your life. When you encounter racism, sexism, ableism, or the myriad of other ways that people suck, we hope you will do something. It will be tempting to give in to apathy or the belief that you are just one person, unable to make a difference. I get that, but please remember that it is through many people consistently stepping up and out against injustice that real and sustained change can happen.

Exactly how you choose to do this will vary depending on the situation. Sometimes you will be asked to respond with immediacy, placing your body in the place to confront whatever injustice is taking place. At other times you will be challenged to act in order to dismantle institutional and structural oppression. Whatever tactics you choose to fight injustice, there will always be people who would prefer that you stop rocking the boat; do not listen to them—rock away.

Only you will know the whats, whens, and hows of reacting to injustice. Trust yourself, be wise, trust those you respect to guide you, and always err on the side of justice.

Rule #71: Be realistic about your skills (Dad)

When I die and you are trying to figure out what should go on my tombstone, if you can't think of anything and your mom nixes "#BRizzle: his game was strong!" feel free to go with "Bruce: he was proudly mediocre at a great many things."

At around fourteen years old, I realized that my dream to play shortstop for the Oakland Athletics was probably not going to happen. Not only was I not big or strong enough but also I was nowhere near talented enough. I was not awful, and with enough practice, money, and opportunities, I could have played for a community college in a very small town—that was going to be it. I love baseball, but I have no delusions about my skills. The same can be said for my guitar playing, my knitting, my photography, and so on and so on. I enjoy these things, but I am unapologetically mediocre at them.

Too often our culture has a "If you are going to do something, be the best!" mentality. Newsflash: not everyone is skilled enough or has the drive to be the best. This is not permission to never try things or to give up but a reminder that this mindset can be dangerous and set you up for failure. The pursuit of greatness can also cause you to prioritize the wrong things and miss out on activities, ideas, or experiences that are a better fit for you.

I firmly believe that there is greatness in all of us, but we cannot all be great at all things. So, go! Embrace your mediocrity so that you can discover and unleash your greatness!

Rule #72: Practice, practice, practice (Dad)

In order to gain proficiency and comfort in any aspect of life, you must be willing to try, fail, learn, and try again. From learning to travel the world without getting lost to making new friends to mastering the art of live-snake juggling, you won't get good unless you work at it.

There will always be the "naturals," who seem to just be good at something, but even they reach a point where, without practice and commitment, they will hit a ceiling. As you discover passions in your life, here are some thoughts on practice.

Athletics. You may not be built for olympic- or professional-level sports—again, sorry for the short genes—but if you want to reach your potential for athletics in tennis, soccer, swimming, or even cliff diving, it's all about muscle memory, which requires repetition, practice, and commitment.

Writing. As you must strengthen your body's muscles for athletics, you must do the same for your mind's muscle for writing. Reading as much as you can and writing all the time are the best ways to become a better writer.

Speaking. Being a good speaker requires being comfortable in your skin, being able to effectively communicate a story, and being willing to try. There will always be nerves, but like playing sports and writing, the more you do it, the easier it gets.

In the end, this is not about being "the best" at something but about finding something that you love and then finding joy in discovering and unleashing your potential.

Rule #73: Live in another city (Mom)

I've been blessed with the opportunity to travel often in my life, but visiting somewhere new and living somewhere new are two totally different experiences. Tourism is one thing, but I am talking about grocery shopping, having water cooler chats, going to church, riding the local transit, and living in a different domicile with different people.

Most summers I would go with my grandma to Molino, Florida, a tiny hamlet just outside of Pensacola. Life in this farming and lumber town was far different than it was in suburban New Jersey or California. Accents were different, dirt was red, phone numbers only had five digits, and the ants would eat you alive. I befriended the girl across the street, and through eating supper, going to ice cream socials, swimming in the swimming hole, fishing for catfish, and being bored in the country together, I was pushed past my comfort levels many times.

Through these experiences I got to know and love people vastly different from those I was usually surrounded by at home. By living somewhere new, I started to form an understanding of how many things I took for granted in my daily life and that not everyone had or did what I was used to.

So, my dearest children, I will happily loan you out at length to Lola, to Montreat, to aunties, to uncles, and to good friends so that you too may learn through experience about the very different ways that so many different people live.

Rule #74: Know your neighbors (Dad)

It is important to know the people who live around you. While there is the obvious "Can you accept a package for me?" type of assistance, knowing your neighbors will also come in handy when you need help jump-starting your car, looking for your runaway puppy, or keeping an eye on your kids when you are out of town—not that we have ever done that.

Wherever we have lived, we have made it a point to know our neighbors. From neighborhood association meetings on crime and violence, to neighborhood garage-sale planning groups, to checking on one another after the 1989 Loma Prieta earthquake, we have always connected with our neighbors.

It seems that we are living in an increasing state of isolation and clustering. This furthers social and political disconnects and can let us miss the opportunity to make human connections that help us see the world through different eyes. In our neighborhood over the years, we've hosted holiday parties, grieved over the deaths, and gathered together on the sideway for casual chats about the world, our lives, and the neighborhood. These experiences have given my life texture, and for that I am grateful.

My hope for you is that you don't give in to the pull toward isolation and clustering of thought. Be willing to find connections with your neighbors, commit the time to participate in neighborhood activities, and lend a hand, a wrench, or a cup of sugar.

Rule #75: Change a flat tire (Mom)

There are some things you are unlikely to escape in life: your father's bad jokes, your mother's overly long grammar lectures, your doggies' kisses, and the occasional flat tire.

Perhaps someone else could change it for you, but sometimes you just need to know how to take care of yourself.

1. Before you drive any car, verify that it has a spare and find out where it is. Make sure you have a jack and a lug wrench. (I learned this one the hard way.)
2. If you get a flat, pull over somewhere safe.
3. Use the wrench to loosen (not remove) the lug nuts. These are always *really* tight. Careful jumping on the lug wrench might be required — be creative.
4. Use the jack to lift the car off the ground. Never, ever get under the car with the jack up.
5. Remove the nuts. Keep track of your nuts! Be sure not to lose the nuts! (Stop giggling. Yes, I said nuts.) Take the tire off the car.
6. Put the spare on the car and tighten the lug nuts by hand.
7. Lower the jack to put the car back on the ground.
8. Make the lug nuts as tight as you can with the wrench. It is good to do opposing nuts instead of going around in a circle. (Yes, I said nuts again.)

Next up: using jumper cables, assembling IKEA furniture, and remembering your #$%&! Netflix password.

Rule #76: Be strong-willed (Dad)

Evelyn took a while to potty train. She told us that she would stop using diapers when she turned four, and on her fourth birthday, she did just that. Our stress, bribery, and pleading were for naught. She decided when it would happen. Not us.

We have always felt that "stubborn" or "hardheaded" to one person was "determined" or "strong-willed" to another. And when you all tested out your own sense of determination, we would say, "This will benefit her when she is older, but right now it's a pain in the ass." No, you were not always angels.

Our hope is that you stay on the determined side of the line so that you experience opportunities that you have earned, your voice is heard when it should be, and you are a full participant in any community of which you consider yourself a part. For when you fail to stand up for yourself, do not claim your space, or silence your voice, you do not honor the gifts that you have to share, and the community is weaker for it.

To be honest, some will deem you arrogant, unwieldy, or rigid when you stand your ground—and you should heed words from trusted people—but as young women, do not let your voice be silenced. Know that you can be determined, confident, and strong while also being humble, kind, and gracious.

Situations will change, other people's expectations will come into play, and you will have your doubts, but never lose your "determined" nature. It will serve you well for a lifetime.

Rule #77: Let it go (Mom)

Sometimes—OK, *often*—you will need to just let it go. "It" may be something you did or something someone else did to you, but sometimes, you just have to do let it go.

"But," you ask, "why let it go, if you still feel it was wrong, if you feel your anger was justified?"

When you don't let something go, it can fester. Anger and frustration circulating around and around in your heart and head can ultimately hurt you more than the object of your anger can. When you rehash something that is in the past or something that you have no control over, you get stuck in an unhealthy cycle of overthinking that can damage your very being. You don't let go because "it" wasn't important; you let go because it's the best thing for you.

Letting go does not mean forgetting or staying in an unhealthy situation. It means breaking the hold that something negative has on you and destroying the power of that memory. It can mean forgiving yourself or creating new patterns of behavior. Letting go can be physical or mental, but it is a change, and change itself can be liberating.

Even though it is a good, healthy change, remember the natural healing process can be painful and uncomfortable in the beginning, but on the other side, you can find healing. Letting go allows you to heal and move forward with your life. When you let something go that is tormenting you, your mind and energy will be freed up for things you can do something about.

Rule #78: Skip school (Dad)

Some of my fondest memories of you growing up are of our "mental-health days," when we took you out of school and played. It might have been a movie, a day trip, or just a day to hang out and run errands—but all included skipping school.

There are two reasons that I made these days a part of your early years. The first is that some days just you and I spent time together. With so many competing activities and commitments vying for our time and attention, these dedicated hours don't happen enough. They may not be grand excursions, but they are cherished times of simply being together. The second reason is that I want you to know that sometimes the best thing you can do to nourish your heart, mind, and soul is to take a break and play. Too often we mistake putting in more time for generating more productivity, when in fact you may need a break to clear your head so you can think better, have more creativity, and in the end be more productive.

Please do not hear this as permission to skip school as a regular event or as an excuse to bail on commitments when things get tough. But do hear it as an encouragement: when things do get tough and stressful, find ways to break up the rhythms of the task, clear your mind, and refresh your spirit. Get out and spend time with those close to you, so you can return refreshed and renewed for the challenges before you.

And if you want to take a mental-health day with your dad, just ask, and I'll be right over.

Rule #79: Understand your privilege (Dad)

We hope that you don't ever forget the nature of privilege in your life. While some feel that each and every person begins life on an equal playing field, and that all one needs to succeed is hard work, we do not believe this to be true.

Hard work is important and your abilities may be worthy of reward, but never believe that you have achieved anything in life completely on your own. There were and are conditions that have given you advantages and access greater than that of others—advantages and access that you did not earn.

A few examples of your privilege:

Shelter. We have a supportive and extensive family structure, so we have never had to worry about being homeless.

Education. The importance of school, study, and exploration has always a part of your life.

Travel. You have traveled to many places—Philippines, Hawaii, New York, Canada, Houston—and this gave you an expanded view of the world in both its beauty and its struggles.

Wealth. While wealth is relative, you have benefited socially, emotionally, and physically because we have been able to afford things like dance classes, club sports, clothes, travel, boba, summer camps, meals out, musicals, and more.

We push on privilege not to make you feel guilty or to say that you should give everything up but to remind you to remember that the playing field is not equal and that out of your own privilege you can and should strive to make it so.

Rule #80: Be grumpy (Dad)

I know that sometimes we have wanted you to just be happy or at least act like you were. For the times that we were unfair in our expectations, we are sorry.

One of the things that you have taught us is that it is OK to be grumpy. While we frown on being rude, allowing yourself to be less than cheery and letting us know that is not a bad thing—in fact, it's healthy. Far too many people put a happy face on everything. They do so because they don't want to burden others with their problems, because they are overwhelmed by feeling down so they overcompensate, or because they see not being happy as a negative reflection on their lives.

Being grumpy is not a weakness to be ignored. In fact, for most of us, it's a daily occurrence that we must learn to recognize and regulate. For some, bad moods are brought on by a lack of food—a.k.a., being "hangry"—while for others of us, it can be stress at work or tension in a relationship; still others have physical things going on that have yet to be addressed or even discovered. Whatever the reason, working through times of grumpiness, bad moods, and even depression means having the courage to admit that happiness is not a constant state of being and that that is OK. Then find the resources, tactics, and practices to help you move through those times.

Hate to tell you, but being grumpy will be a lifelong occurrence, so embrace it, understand where it comes from, and then allow yourself to get to the other side of it.

Add your own...

Rule #81: Fart (Dad)

Everyone does it. Embrace it. Let your fart flag wave!

So as not to embarrass you kids any more than I already have, I'm going to use the dogs as examples when it comes to the art of the butt trumpets. Both Fawn (chiweenie: chihuahua and dachshund mix) and Vespa (English bull terrier) embody the best and worst of acceptable farting practices.

First off, both Fawn and Vespa have healthy and active sphincter sirens and their flatulence can occur at any moment. There is no rhyme or reason to their tooting, only that when their bodies say, "Pass the gas," they oblige. And just as they have differing personalities, each cuts the cheese in unique ways: Fawn's dainty frame emits puffs that are more like teeny tiny hiney hiccups than full-out rump roars, while Vespa's back-end blowouts are loud and proud. And yes, both stink up the place, often clearing the couch area if not the entire room.

But what the dogs do not have a grasp on—and humans should be able to—are the concepts of consideration, discretion, and control. While we don't want to shame anyone about their bodily functions, when you feel one coming on, walk into the other room, open a window, or at least find a corner far away from any breathing life forms. Again, dogs do not have the capacity to understand consideration, discretion, and control, but you, my human daughters, you do.

Now that you know the difference between canine cheek squeaks and human hootie honkers, please fart accordingly.

Rule #82: Feed people (Dad)

When I was growing up, it was not uncommon for me to come home and find that some stranger would be joining us for dinner. While this might sound odd, my mom has always had a generous heart and home. She got this from her parents. I hope you have seen it in your parents, and we hope you too will practice the gift of welcoming—and feeding—people.

The kind of people who have come into our world has varied: single, coupled, old, young. But they all seemed to find something around our table. Not only was the food always plentiful but also my mom's ability to accept people into our community has always been inspiring. In no time, folks find themselves being referred to as "auntie" or "uncle," and the next round of visitors will wonder how they are related to us.

Feeding is not just about nourishment of the body but is also about how we feed the soul and heal the spirit. This can be done by inviting folks who have nowhere to go into your home over the holidays, randomly bringing a meal to people living on the streets, or just receiving people into your life in a way that says, "At this particular moment in time, we're family."

As you welcome people in, they will come and go. Some will become good friends, and you will wonder what has become of others after a time. But what remains are acceptance, generosity, and food—gifts that feed the heart, body, and soul. You will feed people in your own ways, but I do hope you will carry on this the tradition and keep up the feeding.

Rule #83: Touch the corners (Dad)

This rule could also be titled, "Simple ways not to die."

The "Darwin Awards"[3] chronicles some of the less than intelligent ways that people die each year:

- 2002: A man placed his ear on the train tracks to listen for any trains. While he did so, a train came and hit him.
- 2007: A group of metal thieves didn't realize that the steel beams they were stealing held up the ceiling.
- 2012: After spitting out an accidental mouthful of gasoline, a man tried to recover by having a smoke.

Now we may be a little parent braggy, but we're just going to assume that you know better than these folks. Still, in addition to the basics, like, "Don't text and drive," "Be aware of your surroundings," and "Don't wear a seal-meat bikini when swimming in the ocean," here are a few more to remember:

- When crossing the street, always touch the corners. This gives drivers definitive information about where you are. Also make sure you make eye contact before you cross.
- When using a knife, cut away from your body, and for large objects, slice rather than push down on the blade.
- When using a ladder, don't stand on the top step.
- Avoid "death by novel" during an earthquake and anchor your bookshelves to the wall.

Now, go on, and, to quote the '80s cop drama *Hill Street Blues* and Sergeant Phil, "Let's be careful out there."

---

[3] Wendy Northcutt, "The Darwin Awards," accessed May 31, 2016, http://www.darwinawards.com.

Rule #84: Be teachable (Dad)

One of greatest hopes that I have for myself as I go through life in work, faith, and love is not to remain stagnant in who I am. This is a daunting task and one that demands that I be more teachable today than I was yesterday and to be more teachable tomorrow than I am today.

Being teachable is not easy, and on most days, I fail. I like the way I do things. I am good at doing some things. I do not like admitting there may be better ways to do some of the things that I am good at. Oh, and I am stubborn. These are not the best indicators for achieving teachability.

You too, dear daughters, have had your bouts with teachability rejection. On occasion and in exasperation in the midst of our vigorous debates, I've dropped the "You know, your dad just might know stuff" card—this is usually followed by audible eye rolling. Our parent-child kerfuffles have been around for generations, but some adults never move out of that stubborn "I know best" mode of thinking. What we hope is that you will eventually realize that, be it your parents, your teachers, your colleagues, or *gasp* even your younger siblings or cousins, other people in your life may in fact be able to teach you something about a great many things, and that's awesome.

So be teachable. When it comes to a skill, a belief, or an attitude, be open to the possibility that you may have room to grow and that there may be trusted and caring people around you who are willing and able to help you do so.

Rule #85: Chill your onions (Dad)

I must admit that, up until this point, I have not done the best job at teaching you how to cook. Other things in our lives have taken up time and squeezed out moments for cooking lessons, and well, I hate to admit it, but you will probably learn most of your cooking once you are on your own.

While trial and error are part of the learning curve, let me offer a few cooking hacks to make things a little bit easier.

- **Chill your onion.** To avoid tears when chopping onions, chill the onion first. It's apparently sciencey.

- **Sharpen your knives.** Dull knives mangle food, waste time, and cause injury, so sharpen frequently.

- **Roll your bacon.** To make strips of bacon easier to separate, roll and unroll the package a few times.

- **Smash the garlic.** Take your clove and, with a wide blade, smash it down. The skin will peel off with ease.

- **Bubble the oil.** To see if any oil is hot enough, dip in the end of a wooden chopstick. If it boils, it's ready.

- **Spin the ketchup.** To get the last drops, with the lid secured, hold the bottom of the bottle and spin it in big arm circles. The ketchup will be forced to the neck.

- **Present.** Always make your meals look pretty. Be colorful, use garnish, and make it look good.

There are so many more things that you will learn on your own, from the internet, and from any future kitchen compadres, but I hope this list will help you to get started.

Rule #86: See color (Mom)

When well-intentioned Americans say, "I don't see color," they are usually saying one of the following things: (a) I don't want to admit there is still racism around me, or (b) I am not comfortable talking about the experiences of brown people.

Disclosure: I was once of those well-intentioned people.

Color is often one of the first features we notice about someone, whether we want to admit it or not. Seeing and recognizing different skin, eyes, and hair is nothing to be ashamed of—babies notice racial differences. It is an honest observation of difference or sameness, known or unknown. Please don't deny these observations; embrace them. However, you also need to understand that, in our culture, people's experiences vary and that sometimes life experiences are closely tied to color, culture, or race. Take the opportunity to see the person you are talking to—really see them. Listen to their story. Appreciate their experience. Honor their identity. See their color as a part of who they are.

Racism is pernicious and insidious. Denying the existence of racism will not eradicate it, and claiming a colorless world that does not exist shows willful ignorance of reality, careless indifference to those who experience racism, and reinforcement of racist structures.

What we all need to say is, "I see you as you are, and I honor your experience of life as I honor my own." Then we all need to act on those words.

Rule #87: Go camping (Dad)

You all have been camping since you were old enough to understand the joy that is eating roasted marshmallows for breakfast, lunch, and/or dinner. It is only fair to let you know that what defines "camping" is highly subjective.

Some might think us city-slicker glampers for the collection of inflatable mattresses, tent heaters, and kitchen equipment that constitutes our compound, and others think we are hippie tree-huggers because we go a full day without a shower. Undoubtedly the truth of our camping street cred is found somewhere in the middle. In the end, the importance of camping lies in the experience of being out in the nature, where you can do things that you would not otherwise get to do.

Whittle. I can remember the sparkle in each of your eyes when you were first handed a knife and allowed to carve wood. Stay in touch with your inner tool-building, caveperson self.

Fish. The whole worming thing was a line that not all of you crossed, but each of you did fish. Keep at it, and someday you'll catch the one worth telling your friends about.

Start fires. You all know how to build a good fire, so don't let any boys or Boy Scouts tell you otherwise. Build. Fire. Good.

Feast. Food = fun, so make sure there is always enough food for breakfast, lunch, dinner, midday breakfast, postlunch, gametime snacks, prebreakfast, et cetera.

Alrighty, for our next trip, you pack the marshmallows, chocolate, and graham crackers—I'll bring the knives!

Rule #88: Be a joiner (Dad)

Working with other people is hard—or, put another way, working on your own is easier. Groups can be frustrating, and just doing things on your own can often be faster.

At the same time, if you only work on your own, you may miss out on some amazing opportunities. Whether it is a school or work project or even a new social group, please step on in. You may discover that the positives and benefits of being part of a group far outweigh the frustrations and difficulties.

Collaboration. As amazing as you are, you do not know everything. The more different minds are involved, the better chance you have of solving a problem or planning an adventure.

Diversity. One of ways you better understand yourself is by getting to know different people. Diversity can be racial, cultural, geographic, sexual, and so on, but regardless, the more you know about others, the more you will know yourself.

Discovery. With more perspectives present, you are more likely to learn something new about the world, your community, and yourself, so let yourself be surprised!

Friendships. *The* best part about being part of the group is the bonding that takes place over common passions and experiences. While you may be amazing and magical, it's nearly impossible to meet new people if you are alone.

As daunting as it may seem, and with a world that shouts, "Be an individual!" I hope you will have the courage and the humility to join new groups and see what can happen!

Rule #89: Be scrappy (Mom)

Scrappiness literally means "made of scraps," with a side order of pugnacious spirit. Why would a parent who endorses nonviolence also endorse pugnaciousness? Well, because the world is the way it is. If you need scrappiness, it means you aren't the favorite; you are the underdog. But those who are scrappy jump into the fray anyway, and they have a chance to win by the sheer dint of their conviction.

I'm sorry to tell you, my girls, but in many things you will have to be scrappy just because you are female. Although we have made progress, we are still a long way from equality. I encourage all girls to embrace their scrappiness. Call it what you will: grit, stubbornness, or scrappiness. It will serve you well.

The important battles in life are often ones that demand scrappiness. Righteousness and justice are only seen in glimpses around the world here and there, and there are great and powerful forces working to keep them from spreading. Fighting for the rights of the oppressed is a fight for the underdog; those who fight for justice and fairness must be willing to jump into the fray, even though success looks unlikely.

Scrappiness isn't fun. Scrappiness isn't glamorous. The scrappy hero of the story is always beat-up and dirty but sometimes, sometimes, also victorious. Fight for your convictions tenaciously, even when you are told over and over you can't win, you're too weak, you aren't smart enough, or you are too cute or too small. Sometimes you will win.

Rule #90: Pamper yourself (Mom)

Pampering is a wonderful gift when it's occasional. For example, when you've lived for a whole week with only twenty bucks for food (see rule #89), and you find three dollars in a pocket, don't save it for something practical—go ahead and indulge on an ice cream if you want it. Of course, if you do it all the time and come to expect it, that is called being spoiled, not pampering. Don't do that.

Pampering reenergizes, restores, and revitalizes our bodies, minds, and souls—something we all need at times. So if your spirit or your body is tired or hungry, even if you don't have the time or money for it, let yourself:

- Sit on the couch and read for a while.
- Take a day off of school or work.
- Have that soda, ice cream, or bubble tea.
- Take a nap.
- Let one responsibility go.
- Take a warm bath.
- Chat with a friend you've missed.
- Call your mom. :-)

Little breaks have a great effect. Of course you should set your bar high and hold yourself to high standards but also allow yourself to be human. Pampering allows you to break the cycle of stress that we so often suffer under and acts as a reminder that we are not invincible. So take a break and pamper yourself—you will be better off if you do.

Rule #91: Send random notes (Dad)

Keep in mind that your dad is not very good at this one, but there is something really sweet about receiving a handwritten note or even an unexpected email or text.

Too many of our relationships these days seem to be transactional in nature: I need something from you, or you need something from me. These are not always bad things, but in a world where we are overly obsessed with purpose, productivity, and deliverables, these kinds of interaction do begin to set up the expectation and suspicion that people only interact if there is something at stake. We are losing the art of communicating for the sole purpose of building relationships, and I implore you to fight the trend and send a random note.

Here a few examples:

Text your sister. "Hey, sister, I'm [insert what you're doing]. What are you up to? Oh, and Dad is awesome."

Send a card to your grandmother. "Dear Grandma, How are you? [Say something about school, soccer, or life.] What are you doing these days? Oh, and my dad is awesome."

Email your mom. "Mom, just wanted to thank you for giving me life. Love you! PS: Isn't Dad really awesome?"

It is easy to forget to send random notes, because they are not driven by deadlines or projects. Do what you need to do to remind yourself, but do send them. The joy you express, the connections you make, and the relationships you strengthen are worth the time. And yes, your dad is totally awesome :-)

Rule #92: Be spontaneous (Dad)

On of my fondest memories of your great-grandma Reyes was when she would show up at our house at eleven thirty p.m., car running, and declare, "Get your stuff; we're going to Reno!" We would all hop in the car; make the four-hour drive to Reno, where the adults would gamble and I would play video games; and eight hours later make the four-hour drive home.

Yes, Grandma Reyes was crazy in the best of all ways. She taught me many things through her words, her actions, and plain ol' osmosis. One of the most important things that she taught me was to be spontaneous and enjoy life.

As a child, I didn't really think about how chaotic this must have been for my mother. Did we never have plans for the next day? Eight hours of driving, seriously? A little warning? I still can't believe that we did this—multiple times.

While my mom might have struggled with these questions, I can't remember a time when we didn't get up and go. Maybe we were scared to tell grandma no, or maybe we really didn't have anything going on; whatever the case, whenever I think about all of the reasons why we can't do something even a little spontaneous, I think back to these Reno adventures. They are not only a reminder of Grandma Reyes's colorful outlook on life but also an ongoing challenge to make sure that we enjoy as much of it as we can.

OK, let's get in the car. Where to today?

Rule #93: Be deliberate (Dad)

I get into trouble by reacting too quickly to a situation—firing off an email in anger, jumping into a project without first thinking it all the way through, or trying to force my timeline onto a difficult situation, only to make things take longer.

The ability to react quickly to situations is a vital skill, but there are also times when deliberation and restraint may be needed. Hitting pause is often be the most effective thing to do.

Lessen anxiety. If you find yourself in a group of people who are going through a stressful situation, sometimes the best thing you can do is to be a nonanxious presence that communicates calm and points out that the situation can be addressed if things are thought through before responding.

Avoid obstacles. When planning something for a group, it's best to understand the many possible hiccups that you might face. You will always run into unexpected bumps, but being as proactive as you can will give you the best chance of not getting overwhelmed by them.

Help people accept your ideas. Be they coworkers, family, or friends, the more people know ahead of time, the better. People generally respond negatively to surprises, so the more you can share and prepare ahead of time, the less resistant folks will be.

When confronted with the choice between "react now" and "be deliberative," the choice is not always clear, but know that both are valuable and essential skills to nurture and utilize.

Rule #94: Put your bras in a bag (Dad)

You would be surprised at how many folks leave home without knowing how to do their laundry. We hope that this will not be you. Not only is doing laundry simply a good hygienic habit to develop but also being able to do it is one more way you can assert your own independence and create a place of home. Here are a few tips:

Separate lights and darks-ish. OK, separating lights and darks is a good idea on the off chance that you have dark clothing that will bleed. That said, you generally don't have to. Not only will you save water but you'll save time.

Put your bras in a bag. Anything with clasps, exposed Velcro, or cords should be put in a mesh washing bag. This lessens the risk of snags, tears, twisters, and other damage that can happen during the washing cycle. Oh, also empty your pockets and unroll your sweaty, gross soccer socks.

Hang dry when possible. Your mom has won me over on this. If you have a place to do it, you will save energy, and your clothes will last longer. Tip: snap out the wrinkles of your shirts before hanging them to save ironing time!

Fold your clothes. While the pile system may be easier, I have found that folding is not only catheric but also helps keep your clothes looking neat—and, when put away, findable.

Keep it simple. Wash in cold and don't use fancy scents and softeners. You and Mother Nature don't need them.

Hope this helps!

Rule #95: Say thank you (Mom)

Saying please or thank you is a small and simple action but one with a profoundly positive effect.

I teach customer service, and a big part of that class is about the importance of simple acts of politeness. Saying thank you communicates more than just gratitude. It can say:

- I know you didn't have to do that, and I really appreciate that you did.
- I acknowledge the time and effort you put into completing what I am thanking you for.
- Wow, that is just what I needed right now.
- I value your help.

Thank you is a way to build up relationships; it is a way to acknowledge each other's humanity and that we are all in this together. Don't offer it just to get thanks back. Don't offer it to make yourself look good. To be worthwhile, saying thank you is one of those gifts that must be given freely and without any expectation of reciprocation.

Sometimes the occasion or the action calls for more than a few words, though. There are times that writing should actually be employed. This act is often known as "sending thank-you notes." The fact that your dad and I are utter failures at modeling this and have *not* done a good job at teaching you this does not mean it isn't important.

However you do it, always recognize what is given to you or done for you—be sure to say thank you.

Rule #96: Pack your patience pants (Dad)

You know that every time we have traveled, at some point or another during a flight delay, one of us says, "OK, everyone, put on your patience pants."

You know what it's like to see people lose their cool: yelling at gate agents, snapping at loved ones, and otherwise being overcome with anxiety, stress, and frustration. While immediate resolution would be great, sometimes these kinds of reactions make the delays even worse. In fact, being a calm presence in the face of such frustration can help to lower the anxiety of the room, helping those around you to breathe a little more easily and possibly move things along.

Other places you may need to break out the pants:

- Grocery store checkout counter behind someone buying their groceries for the year
- ATM behind someone making many transactions
- Stop-and-go traffic that is more stop than go
- The car in the driveway, waiting for the rest of the family to hurry up and get in the car

In the end, there are some things that are simply not worth getting worked up about. Sure, sometimes there will be injustices to confront, but for the times when delays, interruptions, and other inconveniences are out of our control, put on your patience pants and, if you need to add to the ensemble, your composure cardigan, your serenity socks, and your "take a deep breath" top hat.

Rule #97: Make hearts on the wall (Dad)

Note: notice that I did not say draw or paint hearts on the wall. This is a crucial thing to remember, especially if you are feeling creative at someone else's home.

The heart that I'm referring to is one that Abby created out of our family photos after seeing someone make a floor-to-ceiling heart shape out of pictures. She had no reason to do it this. It was not a school assignment, and we didn't add "make huge heart out of old pictures" to the family chore list. She was just bored. She saw it, thought about doing it, and did it.

We all need spontaneous and creative endeavors that can help refresh our souls. Here are three components of this project that I think may help us unleash future creative projects:

See it. You were open to seeing something that touched you somehow. *Seek out and remain open to new things.*

Create it. You thought to yourself, "I can create that," without hesitations or fear. *Be bold in your creativity.*

Finish it. You made sure it was not too big for your time, and you finished it. Not every project has to be done big. *Keep taking on small, creative projects that you can finish.*

Like the "heart on the wall," we all need random and unassigned creative outlets that are life-giving and that do not require a huge amount of investment in finances, time, or energy.

Thanks, Abby, for the reminder. Now to discover my own heart on the wall—and then make it!

Rule #98: Practice nonviolence (Mom)

At first glance, nonviolence looks like an absence of something, but it is not. It is the presence of wholeness, of knowledge, and of spirit. It is an immovable belief in the rightness of your cause. It is active resistance to that which is wrong. Nonviolence is powerful, and because of that, it demands great courage of us.

You've studied some of the greatest examples of nonviolence: Mahatma Gandhi in India, Rev. Dr. Martin Luther King Jr. in the United States, Nelson Mandela in South Africa, and perhaps the longest nonviolent struggle for rights, the suffrage movement. I hope that nonviolence becomes much more than something you learn in a textbook but will become part of you. Don't let these examples intimidate you. In your lifetime there will be many opportunities to choose nonviolence:

- The other team's players smack your arm instead of giving high fives at the end of a soccer game.
- Students at school want to set up a practical joke that could cause real harm.
- Social media contacts begin bullying someone online.
- Protesters are being beaten at a demonstration.

Remember, nonviolence is a practice; you have to use it to help yourself grow better at it. Often the temptation for flight or retaliation is strong, but building up a practice of nonviolence in the smaller daily struggles will give you the strength and confidence to use it when your cause is even greater.

Rule #99: Be PC (Dad)

At some point in your life, as you express your beliefs and challenge people on their words, you will be dismissed as being "politically correct." When these accusations come, we hope you will be a bit surprised, because what we have taught you to see what some call political correctness as "knowing that words have power and can impact others more than you know."

Yes, sometimes you may find it silly or annoying when we talk about saying "humanity" instead of "mankind" or when we remind you about language that others may deem offensive, but what we hope you hear is that the words you use are important. How people talk about women, people of color, or folks in poverty is important because our words can either perpetuate division or build people up.

Put another way, if you hear that a phase or term makes folks uncomfortable or pains them in some way, you will need to decide if that reality will influence the language you use in the future. Sometimes it will feel like you have run out of words, sometimes messages will be conflicting, and sometimes you simply will not understand the reaction. At those times, breathe and trust that you have the creativity and mindfulness to expand your vocabulary and use your words to build up others, or at least not participate in tearing them down.

In the end, being PC is about hearing the discomfort of another and deciding if you care enough to change.

We hope you will.

Rule #100: You'll trip. You'll fall. You'll be OK. (Mom)

he·li·cop·ter par·ent: *a parent who takes an overprotective or excessive interest in the life of their child or children.*[4]

I fear that the rise of helicopter parenting in my generation has created an ingrained terror of making a mistake in yours. So despite the fact that your dad and I just used up a whole lotta words telling you what to do, we also recognize that you won't always get it right—or even listen at all. Not only is it OK for you to make mistakes, we *expect* it.

Mistakes are part of the learning process; how else could you learn what doesn't work? Mistakes remind us we aren't perfect, which helps us to be more patient when others aren't either. At the wonderful K–8 school you attended, your teachers taught you that mistakes are opportunities for inspiration, and you discovered this truth in your own art. Mistakes are not fun, but they are a part of life, and sometimes life is better because of a mistake. When I met him, I tried to set your dad up with Aunt Debbie. You are the result of how that worked out. I got fired from my first full-time job after college, which allowed me to get my teaching credential, and teaching is my life's calling.

You are loved, you are strong, and you are human. You will trip and fall as you go through life. But you will get back up and dust off your hands and carry on. You will be OK.

---

[4] *Oxford Dictionaries*, accessed June 1, 2016, http://www.oxforddictionaries.com.

Rule #101: Kick 'em in the balls and run (Dad)

Yep, you read correctly. The final rule deals with genitals and violence. We're keeping it classy 'til the end.

We joke around a great deal about actually and metaphorically doing harm and then darting away. In this rule lies our hope that you have enough confidence and courage to claim and cultivate your individuality. In other words, you be every ounce of you—but be sure to stay safe while being you.

There may be a time when you find yourself in a situation where you do not feel safe. We trust that in most cases you will be able to find an exit, but if you ever find yourself in physical danger, do anything and everything you can to escape: scream, gouge eyes, bite arms, scratch faces, or, if applicable, forcefully send a foot, knee, or fist to the groinage area—repeatedly.

And then there will be times when you find yourself in a situation that feels emotionally confining. Maybe a coworker is being a jackass, you are fighting with a friend, or a family member is being super annoying. If the alternative is to say or do something that you will regret later, when really all you need is some space, you have our permission to metaphorically hurt them and leave. Keep in mind that you may be the object of such internal outbursts, so be judicious with your punishment.

While this may be the last rule of this book, as you know, there are more unspoken and assumed ones that we will pull out when convenient. No matter the day, never forget the one rule that binds this entire book together: "Know that you are loved."

Last chance to add your own...

Conclusion, a.k.a., Parenting Is Never Over

Whew. You made it.

Congratulations, your job as parents is totally complete. Book that trip to Hawaii, say farewell to parental responsibility, and get yourself ready for a life of shave ice, sunny beaches, and Kahlua pork. Mmmmmm.

cheek slap (metaphorically, of course)

Wake up, Bruce and Robin, you're dreaming. Again.

OK, we all know that there is never really an end to being a parent, but there are certainly days when we wish there were. It is OK to think this. We all do. For as wonderful as parenting is, it's tiring, and knowing that it's never over makes it feel all the more life consuming. Self-care and tending to your health in body, mind, and spirit are imperative and will help keep you refreshed and energized for the journey. For as tiring as being the parentals of our three daughters has been, the gift that is parenting in its many forms is one that has provided us with so much life, love, and laughter.

While parenting is not for everyone, our lives are fuller for having been parents to Analise, Abigail, and Evelyn.

If you are finishing this list for the first or the fourth time, we hope that we have made it clear that some of the most rewarding aspects of parenting are the pokes, prods, and pleadings for each of us to adapt and change and to encourage and make space for others to do the same. Just as we have done our best to create space where our kids can grow and mature, we as parents have also changed and shifted as our children created chances for us to do likewise. This natural growth of body, mind, and soul provides all involved with an opportunity to more fully grow into the people whom we are called to be and become.

Such a gift. What an adventure.

As we approach the end of this handbook, we leave you with a few last thoughts about some of the transitions in life. In these final paragraphs, we offer our hopes, our experience, and our encouragement for the many endings and beginnings you will share with the children in your world.

Embrace growth for all. We discovered early on that all three of our daughters were liars. When they were around three or four years old, we asked each of them if they would agree to stop growing up and stay three or four years old forever. We often had to negotiate a higher age, as they each wanted to at least go to school, but to a child, when they hit the agreed-upon age, they did *not* stop growing up.

And we pinky promised.

We told you—liars.

Obviously, your children will keep growing up as well, but so will you as parents. Central to your family relationships is allowing them and yourself to do so. As individuals and as a family unit, we hope you will try new things, risk failure, and discover new passions, and all the while revel in how everyone grows and thrives. Sure, there will be moments of tension and conflict as people make choices and live—a.k.a., the "What the hell were you thinking?" moments—but even through the tough times, when they're handled well, beauty can emerge on the other side. Growth is often challenging to embrace and sometimes difficult to watch, but we choose to believe that, with mutual acknowledgment, support, and patience, parents and children can become more fully human when each gives room for the others to do so.

Remember, you can't keep them or you from growth, even if you do pinky promise.

Celebrate rites of passages. There are so many amazing transitions in life, both in childhood and in adulthood. And while you certainly don't want to be frivolous with your celebrations and parties, acknowledging and celebrating major and minor milestones in life are important:

- Baptism, dedication, or communal birth rite
- First day of school
- First period
- Turning thirteen
- Turning sixteen
- Driver's licence
- First job
- Turning eighteen

- Graduation from high school
- First job
- Moving out of the house
- College graduation or adult milestones

Marking these moments allows us all to experience community in support and accountability. Rites of passage build individual identity, build awareness of and connections with the world, build confidence of spirit, and increase depth of emotion.

Someday the roles will reverse. As our own parents age, the idea that at some point the child becomes the parent and the parent becomes the child begins to ring very true.

We have seen and can expect that this transition is one of the most difficult—nay, excruciating—transitions in the parent-child relationship. A child must now care for and protect the one who has always been the caregiver and protector; the one who has always protected and cared for must now accept care and protection. At the worst points, parents can be greatly resistant when they feel their independence slipping away, and in the same vein, children find themselves feeling burdened with the responsibilities of caregiving during what can be some of the most chaotic times in their own lives. These are hard times, filled with painful realizations and difficult decisions. There are feelings of loss, distrust, anger, and grief. For everyone's emotional health, it is important to remember that experiencing this range of emotions is normal and should not be a cause of shame or guilt.

But just as this era can be a strain on the relationship, it also provides an opportunity for letting go, exploring new areas of life, and strengthening of the parent-child bond. It is in these times when stories can be passed down from generation to generation. This is the time for building upon the richness of experiences shared, learning stories never shared before, and even repairing past transgressions and experiencing healing.

As we said at the beginning of our journey, this book was not intended to be a dispensary of foolproof parenting tips. And while it feels as though we have touched upon as much as was parentally possible in this handbook, we know that there are plenty of areas to cover that we didn't address. There will always, always, always be new things to learn, perspectives to tweak, and actions to rethink as the adventures of parenting progress. We hope that we have given you the courage to let go of guilt, self-doubt, and unrealistic expectations while also challenging you to be and do better as a parent and a person.

And finally, please take to heart that people have been doing this parenting thing for a very, very, very long time. Not every parent throughout history has done a stellar job, but we choose to believe that most have done the best they could. We also choose to believe that even those who seem to be the worst examples of parents, at the center of their beings, have acted out of love. And while it doesn't give permission to be a crappy parent, loving your child, first and foremost, is all we can ask.

Thanks for joining us on the journey, and welcome to the fight against asshattery!

SISTERS, 2014

Extra Gravy

Who doesn't like a little extra gravy?

What you will find in this section are some extras that we felt folks might be interested in. Among other things, we've included some pictures of our smiling faces, some background on this project, and letters to expectant parents, our daughters, young Bruce, and young Robin.

Thanks again for joining us, and enjoy the extras.

Keep in Touch

If you have any questions or suggestions, or if you want to tag us as you read, share, and encourage your friends to buy their own copies, let's stay in touch—no pressure, though.

Links to #DontBeAnAsshat Book:

- Twitter: twitter.com/2dontbeanasshat
- Instagram: instagram.com/2dontbeanasshat
- Amazon: http://amzn.to/1TZFqZh
- Authorgraph: http://goo.gl/DBluRx
- Store: reyes-chow.com/dontbeanasshat

Bruce is @breyeschow on most social networks:

- Website: reyes-chow.com
- Twitter: twitter.com/breyeschow
- Instagram: instagram.com/breyeschow
- Facebook: facebook.com/breyeschow
- Snapchat: snapchat.com/add/breyeschow

Robin is @robin_pugh on most social networks:

- Twitter: twitter.com/robin_pugh
- Instagram: instagram.com/robin_pugh
- Snapchat: www.snapchat.com/add/robin_pugh

Buttons, Stickers, and more
reyes-chow.com/dontbeanasshat

A Letter to Expectant Parents from Us

First and foremost, congratulations!

Somehow, someway, a child is already part of or soon will be entering your life. Let that soak in just a bit, and then repeat after us: "Holy crap!"

Yes, you are now responsible for raising said child.

Take a deep breath.

And exhale.

We bet you were wondering when you would receive your official parenting handbook—many thanks to whomever gifted this copy you! By now we hope that you have come to the realization that you were more prepared and studied when you received your driver's license, adopted a puppy, or stood in the produce aisle about to take the plunge and choose the ripest watermelon.

And in all honestly, you probably were.

But never fear; we are here to assist you in this new endeavor because thumping them on the head may be a good way to choose melons—but not so much for raising kiddos.

This is probably a good time to remind you that we offer neither any "guaranteed to work or your money back" parenting tricks nor a big-ass bag of magic parenting fairy dust that will be waiting for you when you get home. Sorry. What we have given you is this, our version of an official handbook, a resource filled with general ideas to keep in mind as you navigate your way through this new world of parenting. So as you digest and translate what you have read thus far, let us offer you a few direct words of encouragement, caution, and perspective.

Good parenting is indoctrination done well. At the risk of starting off by sounding a bit uptight, "Whatever" is not a good parenting strategy. Yes, you must pick your battles, and yes, each child must be given room to explore the world and develop their own opinions, but you, dear parents, have the primary responsibility to build the foundations upon which your child will then build their beliefs and behaviors. Don't be afraid to pass on those things that you believe are important: traditions, passions, ideals, and perspectives.

Sure, at a certain point children will rebel against the awesome wisdom that you are attempting to bestow upon them, but having a base against which they can push and which they can measure against other possibilities is better than giving them nothing at all.

Now if you are passing on right-wing ideals, you never cry at movies, or you are a New York Yankees fan, then please, yes—you should totally go with the "Whatever" parenting method.

Children are not projects to complete, destinations to reach, or recipes to prepare. We all want the best for our kids, and we want to offer them guidance. That said, when we cross the line from to parent to programmer, treating a child like an automaton that, if coded just right, will grow up to be a brain surgeon, middle school teacher, or professional yodeler, we can unintentionally block them from discovering passions and skills that exist beyond our own scope of experience. Sure, you may not actually want them to discover new vocations and avocations, but if you wish to have child who finds fulfillment and joy in what they do and in who they become, forcing them down a predefined and rigid path might not be the best idea.

All kids are different: personalities, passions, perspectives, and developmental stages. We hate to be the bearer of bad news for those of you who are contemplating multiple offspring. First, really think about this, especially if you are heading toward having three kids, a.k.a., saying, "I give up, chaos, you win." And second, children do not come off of a factory assembly-line, uniform in all aspects of their being.

Sorry.

As we have observed in our kids, practically from their births, it is painfully and beautifully clear that each of our three daughters is distinctly different from the others in almost all facets of her life. Each has found joy and adventure in different things, each has discovered gifts and passions in different activities, and each has required us to be nuanced in how we provide structure, encouragement, and discipline. We have also found that tried-and-true thinking about development stages and how bodies and brains generally work at difference ages and stages of life has been invaluable. (Please see the "Extra Gravy" section on developmental stages.) So they are not quite a blank slate, but as you raise successive children, it is wise to be attentive to the differences that lie within each of them.

All parents are different: personalities, passions, perspectives, and origins. Just as each child is different, each parent is different as well. This is so important to remember because the differences on both sides of the parent-child relationship make each combination a recipe for discovery or disaster. As the grown-up in the relationship, it will be your responsibility to adapt, as you will run up against difficult situations that are more about personality differences than about the situation itself.

For instance, both you and your child may be extremely stubborn, or as we say in our home, "determined." Being strong-willed in and of itself is not bad, but when it turns into a battle of wills, you, the parent, must be willing to change tactics in order to find resolution and understanding. For one child, a stern word may be needed in the moment, but another child may need to take a moment before being able to talk about what happened. It is not their responsibility to always know the best way to proceed; it is ours as parents to discover and then move forward.

To be clear, this is not about giving in or being soft but about being attuned to the particularities of all the personalities so that you can be a help and not a hindrance to yourself on your parenting journey.

Model that which you hope to see in your kids. As we know, the modeling thing doesn't always work. We know far too many conservative Republicans with liberal Democrat kids to believe that kids automatically take on everything that we do.

That said, acknowledging that mirrors can be warped, fogged up, cracked, and sometimes crystal clear, we do think there is some truth to the idea that children are a reflection of their parents. We need to be consistent in our own behaviors so that we create a normalcy around the perspectives and behaviors that we hope to see in our kids. Because we want our kids to understand what it means to apologize, we apologize to them when we are in the wrong. Because we want our kids to embrace nonviolence, we do not spank or or smack our kids as a form of discipline. And because we want them to develop healthy and whole romantic relationships, we do not hide our affection and playfulness from them—plus it's just fun mortifying your children by engaging in a little flirting or kissing in public, where they can see us.

Be the grown-up. There will be times when you will desperately want your toddler or teenager to independently make rational, thoughtful, and regulated decisions. Yes, we must equip them to assume agency, initiative, and independence—all good things—but there will also be situations when we make some choices for them. There will be times when only you can decide what is best for them, and you will have to be the adult then. This goes for everything from determining how long playful and unfocused times last to dealing with public meltdowns to making decisions about their education, activities, and general welfare. How much input your kids have in making these decisions will and should shift and grow, but always remember that you are the parent.

Know how you will discipline. Like so many parenting decisions that need to be thought through, discipline is one of the most important. The ways in which you define boundaries and deal with ramifications for crossing those lines will impact so many areas of your child's life. Understanding developmental stages, individual personalities, and your own disciplinarian tendencies are all vital to make wise and effective decisions about discipline.

To begin, let's play the what-if game. (No, these do *not* come from real-life experiences.)

- What will you do when—when, not if—your child melts down in public, complete with high-pitched wailing, body flailing, and back talk?
- What will you do when—when, not if—your child not only won't follow your instructions but willfully and defiantly continues whatever behavior you are trying to curb?
- What will you do when—when, not if—you catch your child in a bold-faced lie about where they were that day?
- What will you do when—when, not if—your child bites, hits, or kicks another human: child, adult, sibling, parent?
- What will you do when—when, not if—your child fails to follow through on a promise or commitment?

- What will you do when—when, not if—your teenager uses "that tone" and is rude and disrespectful?
- What will you do when—could be if, but c'mon, probably when—[insert your most memorable childhood offenses]?

The easy and condensing answer is "Well, my children will know better"—if you believe this, please see rule #2—but the reality is that even if your perfect child does not live out any of these specific things, there will come a time when you will have to discipline your child for something.

Often times the best thing to do is, after the first—or second, or third—time something happens, try to figure out if there is any way to preempt the behavior. After all, the last thing you want to do is set your child up for failure by placing them in a stressful, tantrum-inviting situation.

When our eldest child, Evelyn, was about two years old, she would throw a nasty fit every time we had to leave a place. What we began to realize is that she did not do well with transitions from one place to another. So when we just walked up to her and said, "OK, let's go," we soon discovered that she was not one of those "she just rolls with it" kinds of kids. In fact, we quickly learned that she was one of those, "Um, honey, why is our child's head spinning around while she is spewing fire from her eyes?" kinds of kids. We only had to go through this three, or four, or eight times before we figured out that maybe there was another way. Yes, we are quick ones.

What we started to do was this: when we were about fifteen minutes away from our planned departure time, we would give her a warning, like, "We are going to leave soon." She was then able to prepare herself for what was apparently a major life change of leaving the park and getting into the car. Who knew these things meant so much to a toddler, but once we figured this out, the tantrums ceased.

There are probably as many ideas for disciplining a child as there are parents, but we found these to be most helpful for those, "What the hell do I do right now?" moments in time:

The "side eye." For infractions in public areas, you must master a look that says, "You had better stop doing whatever you are doing." Note: practice if you must, but do not wield your side eye unless you really have it down. The last thing you want is for your mean look to make them giggle.

The "I am not playing around" voice. It is imperative that you save your serious voice for serious times. A forcefully spoken "That is enough," or a loud, "Don't hug that porcupine!" can nip many a mishap or dangerous situation in the bud, especially when children are out of arm's reach.

The "I'm just disappointed" talk. Sometimes the idea that the child is disappointing their parents, family, community, and self is punishment enough, and little else is required.

The "Do you want me to call Lola?" threat. My personal favorite, also known as the "Fun Dad, Mean Grandma" bit, means that my kids know that if Grandma is mad, they can say good-bye to ice cream for breakfast, having no limits on TV, shopping, and other spoils.

The "You pay for it" ramification. We're flexible on this, but as kids begin to earn money via jobs, allowance, or couch cushions, they are able to be more fiscally responsible for things like lost or broken phones or other property damage.

Other disciplinary tactics include grounding, taking away valued items or making them watch *Star Wars: Episode I—The Phantom Menace* on continuous loop, but what we do *not* do is make empty threats. Bruce was the six-year-old kid who, when his stepfather threatened, "I will stop this car, and you can get out," hopped out when the car stopped and started walking—on the freeway. Bluff. Called. Mic. Dropped. The moral of the story: don't threaten something that you are not willing and able to enforce. Sure, there will be times to be flexible, but if your child knows that, "You're grounded for a week," actually means, "until Dad forgets," the discipline becomes hollow and ineffective.

Another thing that we do not do is spank our children or anyone else's. Yes, we have friends and family who spank their kids—and say they are fine—but we are not a spanking household, and on this we are both in complete agreement. Our children are often playfully threatened with a good beating if they don't promptly deliver a cookie to the couch-sitting parental, but they all know that it will never happen. Some might think that a lack of spanking is just a symptom of a spoiled America; others would say that under no circumstances should an adult strike a child; and some simply think spanking is a cultural choice. Because we think that using violence in response to violence is not a helpful tactic at any stage of life, we have landed firmly in the "we do not spank" camp and have made the choice not to spank, swat, or hit our children with our hands, wooden spoons, slippers, switches, belts, fly swatters, or any other instruments, culturally acceptable or not.

While we feel strongly about the spanking, at the end of the day, discipline, like cosleeping, education, and other parenting choices, is highly contextual. You must take into consideration the parent, the child, and any counsel available—from the school, other caregivers, and the like—and then make the best decision you can.

Let them live their childhood—you've had your chance. This one is hard for all parents. After all, who doesn't want their kids to love something that we love? Bruce likes, no, *loves* baseball, so he has always had this voice whispering in his head, "Please, please, please, one of my daughters, please love baseball." His dreams have manifested themselves to varying degrees, but what he has been pretty good at is not trying to live out his baseball dreams and passions through the girls. For as much as we parents want our kids to love and excel in the activities that we loved and excelled in, it doesn't matter, because we have lived our childhoods, and now we must let them live theirs. From dance, to math, to theater, to sports: be passionate and be supportive, but don't try to be them.

Give yourself a break. In a world with so many expectations placed upon young people, it is the parent's job not only to ease anxiety but also not to add to it. There will always be a level of worry and stress about the choices we make for our kids, but when that rises to the level that our kids begin to pick up on our stress, we have moved to heaping expectations on ourselves that are unfair, unachievable, or both. Yes, each decision that we make has ramifications, some more than others, but that does not mean that every decision should have ulcer-inducing potential.

Seek out, build up, and invest in communities that will nurture your child. You cannot and should not raise your children alone. Some of the greatest assets you have in life are the people around you who can help to broaden children's experience of and exposure to the world. Over your child's life, you will have the opportunity be part of groups where you can find meaningful interactions, develop deep friendships, and practice being community. From youth activities like soccer, Scouts, and summer camps to adult-driven groups like the PTA, church, and parent groups, it is important to invest time and energy in your community in order to mutually influence one another's children in positive ways. In these groups your children can seek and know social familiarity and emotional support when other communities are creating anxiety and stress in their lives. This is also true for parents, so pouring into these groups is good for everyone.

Don't parent other people's kids — usually. There is something deeply spiritual and personal about the relationship between parent and child. This is never more evident than when someone offers unsolicited parenting advice. Generally well-intentioned, often passive-aggressive, and sometimes right on, unsolicited advice gives even the most calm and even-keeled parent the capacity to bite your face off. Barring physically dangerous situations, just take note of those "If that were my child…" conversations that are going on inside your head and do your best to keep them there. Your advice will most likely only fuel the gossip train and create awkwardness at the next PTA meeting.

Parent other people's kids—sometimes. Following up on why not to parent other people's kids, there are times when you should. So many messages in today's culture say, "Don't get involved," "Mind your own business," or "Every person for themselves," but this is a short-sighted approach for a society to take when raising its children. Yes, there are lines not to be crossed, but one of the gifts of being part of communities like public school, Girl or Boy Scouts, and faith communities is that, regardless of status or station, we are committing to the growth of each child, not just our own. Not all people or youth activities have committed to this, so it is vital to take time to seek out and create situations where our children can have respect for and find safety with adults other than us. Spaces like this communicate the idea that the world is not as "dog eat dog" as it seems, and that in order for one person to truly thrive, the rest of the community must also.

Support other parents—always. Never get to the point where you think just because your kids might not act a certain way—or aren't at this particular moment—that you are above dealing with the public meltdown. Dealing with a screaming child in the store, managing an active and handsy toddler at the cafe, or just being consumed by the overwhelming feeling that this parenting thing is too hard—we have all been there. And during these moments, knowing and seeing that there are folks judging us never helps. We can help one another through these times and remove a bit of burden from parents when they are frazzled and overwhelmed. A genuine word of encouragement, a nod of "I've been there, and it's going to be OK," or a gesture like opening a door or lifting a stroller can do immense good for the psyche of any struggling parent. You know what is is like both to be judged and to be helped, so always strive to do the latter.

Let other people parent your child. Trusting someone else with your baby at any age is difficult. This struggle to let go is not only about the physical caretaking of your child but the emotional, spiritual, and psychological aspects as well. And while we do believe that 90 percent of the time parents know their kids the best, there will be times to let go and let others care for our kids. We have always found it helpful to have adults in their lives whom they can trust. This can be anyone, including other school parents, good friends of the family, an aunt, an uncle, or another relative. We want our kids to have another adult perspective to go to when they are struggling, and they also need to have adults in their lives in times of emergency or when they need a ride home from school because their parents forgot to pick them—not that this has ever happened.

When we allow other adults to parent our kids, the adults are reminded of the of the joys and hardships of growing up, the children learn how to navigate the world outside of their immediate family, the parents may learn new things about their children that are only made evident when their children are not with them—and most important, all are given the gift of seeing and experiencing the world in new ways.

Expand their world; don't narrow it. This may be the most influential perspective that has formed our parenting. The world is an interesting and complex place, and while we have certainly had the urge to actually and metaphorically bubble wrap our children's bodies, minds, and spirits in order to protect them from the dangers of the world, we have always felt that our number one job is to help them explore the world and equip them to thrive as they do so. This has to do with pretty much everything: travel, politics, faith, food, culture, art, and activities. This does not mean that we are foolish or that we put them in harm's way—all relative, we know—but it does mean that we see more value in exploring the possibilities than limiting them.

So, there you go. As you begin this journey, we hope these thoughts will give you a good foundation upon which you will begin to build your own style and posture of parenting. It is a lovely journey, so blessings and good luck.

Robin

Bruce

IT REALLY IS FUN, 2014

EASTER, 2014

A Letter to Our Girls from Mom and Dad

As we have laid out the lessons and guidance that we hope to pass on to you, we want you to also know the foundations upon which we have built our understanding of parenting.

Our hope is that you will do you. Our greatest hope for you and your life is that you will discover who you are truly intended to become and not who the world expects you to be. As you go about your life, there will be forces pushing and pulling you in many directions. We hope that we can give you enough confidence to know when you should take your own path and enough humility to know when to listen to the guidance of others. Above all, it is our hope that in all that you do and experience—in the joys, the struggles, the adventures, and the everyday—you will feel good about who you are, who you have been, and who you are becoming.

Our love is unconditional-ish. No matter what happens in your life, what choices you make, or what struggles that you face, please never feel as though you do not have a home you can return to. Know that you will always have a home—physical and emotional—that is safe, where there are arms to enfold you, and with a table to feed you. But to be clear: while the love and support will never wane, it could come to a point in time when living together is not a good idea because of your or our lack of ability to make that work in loving, healthy ways. And yet even if we are not under the same roof, the love that resides in our hearts that will support you whenever and however you need us to.

You have brought us joy. To be honest, being your parents has not always been kicks and giggles—but it has been a journey filled with joy.

A partial list of the adventures of us:

- When four-year-old Abby stealthily tied Evelyn to the chair during Auntie Lauren's graduation—because she was bored
- Annie's game face
- When angry three-year-old Evelyn stormed away and intentionally pooped in her pants because she was mad at Mom
- Annie's belly laughs
- Evelyn yelling at the TV. All. The. Time.
- Abby's giggles
- When we discovered that Evelyn had named most of her dolls and stuffed animals...Evelyn
- Annie's *Starry Night*–inspired painting on her window.
- When Abby was busted standing on the counter while sneaking marshmallows—because Evelyn told her to
- Evelyn's grumpy or monster face

- When Abby and her friend battled for the center-front spot during the first-grade class dance performance
- And finally, according to Annie, "When Annie became swag money in the seventh month of 2003"

Whether you are causing us to feel delight or distress, you bring us joy. We hope you will always know and believe to the depths of your soul that we love being your parents.

May you live with peace. While we do not wish struggle upon you, throughout your life you will be faced with situations that will bring you pain—in body, mind, spirit, and soul. There will be moments when you feel out of control, overwhelmed, and lost, but even in those moments, we hope that you will know peace.

When we speak of peace, we are not talking about the kind of peace that signifies an absence of hard work, struggle, or adversity, but the kind of peace that grounds you as you move through the chaos. If you genuinely know who you are, know you are loved, and know that there is hope, you will have peace.

We love you girls. Thank you for being you.

Mom   *Dad*

Mom   Dad

WOMEN'S WORLD CUP
CANADA, 2015

Dear Twenty-Six-Year-Old Bruce, from Old Bruce

Congrats to you, Bruce of 1996!

Oh, 1996—the "Macarena" is all the rage, Major League Baseball approves interleague play, *Rent* opens on Broadway, *Friends* is beginning its epic run, some company called Amazon starts making waves, and New Edition finally releases their reunion album.

These are the days—and the days before offspring.

Well, my friend, all of that is about to change.

Not only did you somehow find a person who is willing to partner up with you for life but she is open to the possibility of producing and raising offspring with you. Yeah, dude, go kiss Robin. She is pretty awesome.

But now, as the kids say, "This shit is getting real," and you all are having a baby human. Daaaaaaaaaaaamn.

So, here is the thing: you are probably pretty well-prepared. After all, you have three younger siblings and multiple cousins, the communities that have raised you will continue to support you, and yeah, your mom has provided a positive and grounded model for parenting. I have faith that you will do fine. That said, dear Bruce of 1996, now that I am nearly twenty years the wiser, let me offer us a few words of encouragement and wisdom to keep in mind as this adventure unfolds.

Raise strong girls. Yep, three girls.

Contrary to what many would have you believe, this is not a tragic twist of fate that can be cured with the birth of a boy, nor is this some kind of karmic payback for past acts of heartbreak or indiscretion. You simply have girls, and it is wonderful.[5] Sure, there are nuances and challenges specific to raising daughters in the world, but trade for three boys? Not in a million years.

The hardest part of raising girls is that you get a glimpse into the world that women have to deal with: a world that objectifies and sexualizes, a world where there is gender-based pay inequity in the workplace, a world where femininity is equated with weakness, and a world where sexism is still pervasive. It is your job to do everything in your power to provide a counternarrative and encourage your girls to be strong women, equipped to navigate and thrive in the world. There are many ways to do this: support activities where women are taking the lead, don't confine them to "girl" things, allow them the agency to make choices in their lives, and most important, be a good male in their world: one who builds them up,

---

[5] On a three-girl side note, when we were married, because Robin did not take on Reyes-Chow as a last name, it was agreed that girls would have Robin's last name and boys would have Bruce's. So, yep, three girls later, Bruce is still the only Reyes-Chow in the world.

supports their risk taking, and is always learning how to be a better man in the world.

You will be changed; embrace it.

Do not parent with fear. Oh, Bruce, you had a crappy stepfather. Let's call him The Big D. While your mom eventually found the courage to leave him, he parented you for a long time and during your formative years. To pretend that you don't have some of his wicked anger embedded in your DNA is foolish and risks being the kind of physically and emotionally violent parent that he was. So check yourself at all times. Do not parent with fear, intimidation, or threats of physical harm, but at every turn, be sure to parent in a way that creates and nurtures a relationship where your children respect you, trust you, and know that you represent safety, support, and love.

Love them. This does seems a bit obvious, but there will be times when you will rely too much on tricks and tools in order to deal with the stress and struggles of parenting. During these times, remember that the best thing you can do is simply love them. That love will look different depending on the situation and the child. Sometimes it will mean binge-watching cheesy television when stress is overwhelming her; at other times it will be taking her out for a late-night ice-cream run without the sisters; and still at other times, it will mean saying, "I'm sorry. I love you."

It's going to be a wild and wonderful life. Enjoy the ride.

Bruce

Bruce

BRUCE AND ROBIN, 1991

Dear Thirty-Year-Old Robin,

from Wiser Robin

Congratulations, Robin in 1996!

Before I forget, you know those awesome black overalls you wore through the first five months of your first pregnancy? Keep them; they will be back in style in 2016.

You're welcome.

OK, now to the task at hand. I know at this stage you are excited and terrified. You actually never saw yourself as having kids until very recently, and here you are. And guess what—you are going to have three! You are going to love it and love your kids, and you will find them to be your most compelling life's work—at least for the next twenty-five years—and the richest reward.

Here are a few specifics to help you along…

Children are not a competition. You will often find yourself with people who want to compare children. While competitiveness is a natural human trait to which we all fall victim at times, don't let yourself be intimidated by the accomplishments of other people's children. None of your children will walk early, and that is OK. Each will eventually crawl and walk and run and play soccer, or play guitar, or do Afro-Haitian dance. Your eldest child won't be able to read well in first grade. Don't worry, and don't force her too much. Everything will click in the middle of second grade, and she will become one of the biggest bookworms ever. Maybe even bigger than you. Doing something early doesn't mean a kid is smarter or better. Brains sometimes need time before they are ready for a particular task, and it doesn't help anyone to try to force things to happen earlier. Some kids aren't ready to read until they are seven years old, and forcing it on them earlier can actually damage their love of reading in the long term. Be attentive to times when your child is responsive and trying and something still isn't happening. Maybe you should let it go for a while and try again later on.

Don't expect logic from a toddler or a teen. You pride yourself on your logic. It was part of your family culture growing up and part of your scientific training in college. Guess what? When parenting toddlers, and sometimes teens, logic doesn't count for *nothin'*. Long, reasonable explanations are a waste of time for your two-year-old (see the bit about children and competition, above). I know you think it should work—and so you will try to explain things even more carefully—but trust me, it just isn't going to come out the way you think. Stick with short, honest, direct answers, and give up on the idea that you will be able to explain away their anger, frustration, or disagreement with what you have to say. Then pick up your kicking, screaming child and graciously exit the store (toddler version) or quietly command your teen to get in the car and let them stew without interruption all the way home.

Love your kids' community. I'm sure no one is more surprised than thirty-year-old you that in eighteen years you will actually be working on a book about parenting. Right now, you are a little worried about your ability to parent and love your own child because you never saw yourself as a parent. Guess what? Not only will you love your children with your every breath, you will love other people's children too. You will choose to be involved in activities with lots of children, and you will call yourself blessed because of it.

Because your children will have their own interests and passions, you will end up hanging out with people who may not be familiar to you. I know you are an introvert, but open up and get to know them. Embrace newness as each child makes her way. (Spoiler alert: you are going to learn all about soccer, and you are going to love watching soccer. I know, right? A sport! I told you parenthood is miraculous.) It takes more than one or two parents to raise a child. I know it may be trite by now, but the need for a village is real. Expand your children's world and yours by truly participating in the communities they are connected to: school, sports, dance, music, church, robotics—whatever they may be. You will be enriched by the love and care you have for the community of children and parents, and your children will be too.

Be genuinely you. You will be one of the most important people in your children's lives. Don't you think they deserve to actually know you? Yes, be a parent. Yes, be strict when needed; you will have to set and enforce many, many boundaries during your time as a parent, but be sure to be genuine with your children. Don't say something you don't really believe because you think it is what parents are supposed to say to children. Please, please don't take on one of those "parent personas," where the parent only says the perfect thing, and never shows any emotion other than support and encouragement. Now, obviously, you can't communicate with five-year-olds the way you talk to coworkers, but you can communicate in a way that is still an honest expression of you.

For example, by the time the girls are ready to leave home, be sure to talk to them about your opinions on global warming, abortion, marijuana use, sex and birth control, gun control, voting, investing, budgeting, the cost of housing, tattoos and piercings, et cetera, et cetera. Of course, I mean you should have these discussions in parts as they are age appropriate. (Again, see competitive childhood.) If they ask about something you don't think they are old enough to handle, be honest by telling them something like, "That is a very serious question and an important topic. I will talk to you about that, but I think you are a little young right now. Let's come back to it in a few years." Or tell them the part they can understand, like, "Yes, I do think the weather is changing. Grown-ups are trying to figure out what to do about it. We should try to drive less, because more cars is one of the things causing the problem." Being genuine and honest with your children is how you model those attributes for them. It builds trust between you, and it lets them know that they can be genuinely themselves with you.

OK, there you go. Have a wonderful journey.

Remember that you will trip and fall, and you will be OK. And so will your kids.

Good luck!

Robin

FOLLOW
@2DONTBEANASSHAT

Developmental Stages

As we have said before, we are not trained psychologists, and neither of us possesses a degree in early childhood development. That said, we both have enough experience in family and organizational systems and have done a good enough amount of reading that we feel pretty secure in our general understanding of developmental stages.

What do exactly do we mean by developmental stages? This is the idea that certain skills or abilities cannot be developed before other, more fundamental, ones have been achieved.

A common example is that you must learn to walk before you can run. This also includes the understanding that it is foolish to expect a child to do something (running) before the child has developed the fundamental skills (walking) that are necessary for that activity. It also includes a certain amount of faith in the development of those stages and the ways that the body and brain work together. Until a child's brain is ready for walking, talking, reading, or throwing a ball, it won't happen, no matter how much excess pressure we put on the child. As long as the environment with the basic tools and encouragement are there, children will develop these skills when they are ready.

Our parenting experience has really hit this idea home for us. Our oldest child was a late reader. Even though she did extremely well in school and was a voracious bookworm from the age of 7.5 on, up to that point she hated reading aloud to us, and frankly, she wasn't very good at it.

Then, over a period of about two weeks in second grade, she went from not being able to read a picture book to us to reading chapter books on her own. I could practically hear her brain "click" with understanding. It was the right time for her, and we needed to allow that to naturally come about. Yes, we were consistent in our encouragement, but forcing her to sit and read to us more wouldn't have made her a better reader; her brain just wasn't ready for her to read yet.

These stages will impact other activities: potty-training, sleep patterns, physical development, and the ability to absorb, analyze, and make conclusions about ideas and concepts. Each child will be different, so we encourage you to read, talk with the educational professions with whom you have entrusted your child, consult medical folks if you feel that there are other concerns, and remember to breathe.

We will include a resource list on the #DontBeAnAsshat website (www.reyes-chow.com/dontbeanasshat), so please let us know of any good books, articles, or videos that you have found helpful.

The Publishing Process

Writing this book was equal parts invigorating, frustrating, insightful, and soul revealing. Not only did we have to work through different writing styles, patterns, and paces, but we have had to deal with our commitment to use Google Docs, as well as all that goes into taking on this kind of self-driven project. It has been a learning adventure for sure.

This is the second book that Bruce has Kickstarted, so we had some knowledge about the process, the pitfalls, and the possibilities. This does not mean that we always learned from that experience or always always remembered the dangers, but at least utilizing the platform was not all that daunting. We did not reach our initial and extremely ambitious goal, nor did we hit our deadline, but in the end, we were funded, paid our outsourced resources, and had enough left over to buy some cool schwag. The final #DontBeAnAsshat Kickstart project and subsequent updates can be found here: https://goo.gl/WuYwFf.

Because we are a committed Chromebook family, we did the actual writing of the book entirely using Google Docs. While 80 percent awesome, Docs is severely limited in some editing tools: the ability to make a numbered table of contents, the number of pagination options, and a few others things. Laura, our editor; Adam, our cover designer; and Bruce, when formatting for the hard and electronic versions, worked off of Google Docs. We certainly could have saved time if we used more traditional tools and resources, but what fun would that have been? Generally, it was fun figuring out how complete this entire project without using Microsoft Word.

As far as marketing, we'll be relying on word of mouth and the interwebs. There will be no fancy schmancy, specialized #DontBeAnAsshat social media strategy other than the hashtag #DontBeAnAsshat, using www.thunderclap.it help spread the word about the release, and our deepest hope that folks share and tag us all over the interwebs using @2dontbeanasshat on Twitter and Instagram.

While we don't expect this book to make enough money to buy us our island, with Bruce firmly entrenched in the gig economy of the day, we intend for this to help Bruce pull his weight—*Robin, with her regular paycheck, pays for food and shelter while Bruce, through his consulting, speaking, and writing, pays for toys and vacation.*

Please buy the book online, or to get your signed books, stickers, pins, and more, visit reyes-chow.com/dontbeanasshat.

Family Photo Album

WELCOME ANNIE! 2003

Family Pics

THE FAMILY, 2007

THE FAMILY, 2015

Bruce and Robin Pics

THE WEDDING, 1990

STILL CUTTING IT, 2011

Robin Pics

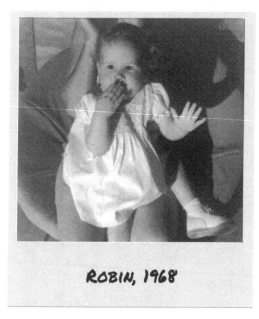

ROBIN, 1968

ROBIN, 2015

Bruce Pics

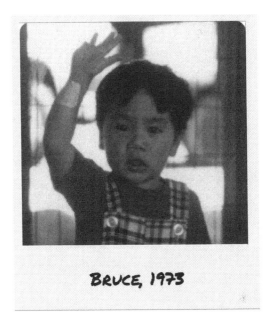

BRUCE, 1973

BRUCE, 2015

Sister Pics

SISTERS, 2007

SISTERS, 2014

Evelyn Pics

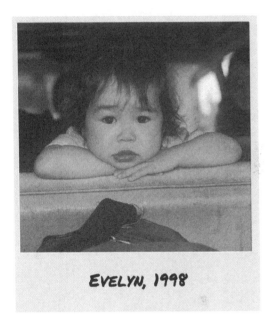

EVELYN, 1998

EVELYN, 2014

Abby Pics

ABBY, 2006

ABBY, 2015

Annie Pics

ANNIE, 2005

ANNIE, 2015

Puppy Pics

Fawn + Vespa, 2015

House of Ears, 2016

Words of Gratitude

There are so many people to thank.

Our grandparents, our parents, and the rest of our big ol' family. There are way too many of you to name, so just know that we think you're awesome and we are grateful for you!

Laura, our editor. Thanks for your patience and ability to help us say what we want to say in a way that makes sense.

Adam, our cover artist. Thanks for your creativity and the cool way that you put the ass on the hat.

Kristin, our proofreader. Thanks for helping to make the whole thing even better with good questions and suggestions.

San Francisco Unified School District and the Rooftop K–8 Alternative School community. Since 2002 you have helped us raise our three daughters in mind, body, and spirit: Ms. Behringer, Ms. Obayashi, Mr. Mayhew, Ms. Cruz, Ms. Kennedy, Ms. Woo, Mr. Kawaii, Mr. Weiss, Ms. Whitcomb, Ms. Contreras, Ms. Vaughn, Ms. Zydek, Ms. Kastner, Ms. Powers, Ms. Looser, Ms. Simpson, Ms. Beaulieu, Ms. Kennedy, Ms. Cooke, Mr. Kehoe, Ms. Hickey, Ms. Kennedy, Ms. Mocklin, Mr. Rogers, Ms. Lathrop, Greg, Christian, Rittinell, Patty, Cyndy, Andi, Amy, Tamra, Joel, Rosalinda, and everyone else!

Leslie and all of the staff of the most awesome Children's After School Arts (CASA) program!

Other educational institutions in our life, Macalester College, Ruth Asawa School of the Arts, and Drew School.

Our soccer sideline family and SF United FC coaches.

The other parents in our kids' lives: Mary and Kayvan, Stephanie, Carrie, Christina, Rick and Kathi, Paul and Gigi, Kara and Peter, Jonelle, and everyone else who has ever fed them a meal, given them a ride, or spoiled them when they needed it.

Our girls: Evelyn, Abigail, and Analise. You have been a gift to our lives. Thanks for your patience and your love.

For the various canine kiddos who have loved us even when our daughters were having second thoughts: Girlfriend, Nala, Sadie, Fawn, and Vespa.

And really finally, the places that kept us nourished: Super Cue Cafe, Philz Coffee, Naan-N-Curry, and La Corneta.

Made in the USA
Middletown, DE
25 June 2016